The First Cities in the World

Anatolia

Çatal Hüyük

Jericho

Mesopotamia

Mohenjo-Daro

Indus Civilization

The Warring
States of China

Series director: Michel Pierre, Professor of History
Art director: Giampiero Caiti
Assistant art director: Jean-Marie Mornard
Editor: Martine Prosper
American project editor: Joanne Fink
English text consultant: Walter O. Moeller, Senior Professor,
Temple University

The publishers would like to thank the following individuals and
organizations for their assistance in the preparation of this book:
Laurence Batigne (for adding color to the drawings); Jamil
Hamoudi, Embassy of Iraq in Paris; The Turkish Bureau of Tour-
ism; The Mexican Embassy in Paris; The Department of Oriental
Antiquities, Musée du Louvre.

Library of Congress Cataloging-in-Publication Data

Coblence, Jean-Michel.
The earliest cities.

(The Human story)
Translation of: Les premieres cites.
Includes index.
1. Cities and towns, Ancient—Juvenile literature. 2. Civilization,
Ancient—Juvenile literature. 3. Middle East—Civilization—To
622—Juvenile literature. 4. Cities and towns, Ancient—Middle
East—Juvenile literature. 5. City and town life—History—Juvenile
literature. 6. City and town life—Middle East—History—Juvenile
literature. I. Deubelbeiss, Patrick. II. Title. III. Series: Saint-Blanquat,
Henri de. Histoire des hommes. English.
CB311.C73 1987   930   86-42656
ISBN 0-382-09214-7

© 1985 by Casterman, originally published in French under the
  title L'histoire des hommes: Les premieres cites.

© 1987 English text Silver Burdett Press.

Published pursuant to an agreement with Casterman, Paris.

First published in the United States in 1987
by Silver Burdett Press,
Morristown, New Jersey.

Photographic Credits

Musée du Louvre - Antiquités orientales (ph. M. Chuzeville):
page 19. Padrol/Explorer: page 20, 21. Delu/Explorer: page 38.
Coll. J. Hamoudi: pages 22, 70. Réunion des Musées nationaux:
pages 26, 27, 28, 36, 43, 46, 48, 49, 58, 71, 72. Hirmer Verlag:
page 30. E. Hattori/UNESCO: page 56. Vautier-De Nanxe: page
66. Mexican Embassy in France: page 65. Archaeological Mission
of Mari: pages 68, 68/69, 69b (2 ph). Gérard Degeorges: page 69t.
Artephot/Bridgeman: page 73. Artephot/Roland: page 75t.
Artephot/Nimattallah: page 75b. Turkish Office of Tourism in
Paris: page 74.

THE HUMAN STORY

THE EARLIEST CITIES

Jean-Michel Coblence
Illustrations by Patrick Deubelbeiss
Translation by Anthea Ridett

Silver Burdett

Morristown, New Jersey • Agincourt, Ontario

CONTENTS

PREFACE

Eight thousand years ago, cities were springing up all over the world, in Mesopotamia, Asia Minor, America, Africa, China, and India. They grew up around temples, markets, grain stores, and crossroads, often close to large rivers whose annual deposits of silt enriched the soil and nourished the crops. The Nile, the Euphrates, the Indus, and the Yellow River brought life to burgeoning civilizations.

For in the cities, with their houses, temples, and large buildings, civilizations were being born. To better safeguard their position, the rich and powerful built palaces of brick or stone, many of which have survived the ravages of time. And to better fulfill the will of the gods and understand the course of destiny, priests built temples for the new religions.

Cities were not only the homes of priests and warriors. There, too, caravans ended their long journeys, merchants and craftsmen plied their trade, and administrators controlled the life of the countryside, the peasants, and their fields. Although wealth came from the land, progress took place in the towns. There, potters, ironworkers, goldsmiths, and carpenters set up their workshops. There the wheel came into full use, on traders' carts and war chariots. And there, most importantly, writing was invented. This major event led to further progress in every direction. It embodied human memory in a new way, and it helps us today to understand a past long buried under the sands, steppes, and forests of the Near East, Asia, and America.

THE FIRST TOWNS

For hundreds of thousands of years, people lived by getting their food from the land and the creatures who lived there. The hunter-gatherers chose to settle in regions well supplied with game and edible plants. If the supply fell short, the hunters would leave, sometimes traveling long distances to seek another home with a more bountiful food supply.

This human adventure story took an all-important turn when people began to cultivate the soil and domesticate animals and gathered together to live in stable, organized communities. This phase of evolution, which lasted for many hundreds of years, led to the development of settlements that steadily grew in both size and number.

Around 8000 B.C. the Ice Age finally came to an end. The climate stabilized, and throughout the planet the human population rapidly increased.

A remarkable ecological balance arose in one particular area, where three continents — Europe, Africa, and Asia — meet, the area that came to be called the Fertile Crescent. Here, people exercised their ever-growing skills in cultivating the soil and controlling and exploiting animal, vegetable, and mineral resources. For the first time, some well-organized agricultural communities regularly produced more food than was needed, which enabled some people to follow pursuits other than hunting and farming. People became craftworkers, making pottery, weapons, and essential tools, all of which were improved tremendously with the discovery of copper, bronze, and, finally, ironworking.

Villages were too small to contain all this newly created wealth. People's natural tendency to group together was intensified, and before long real towns and cities came into being. Their birth and steady growth corresponded to everyone's needs. It was easier to ward off attacks in towns so both individual and collective safety were better guaranteed. Food reserves could be stored in public granaries in the event of destruction of crops by natural disasters. The exchange of goods was made easier by the existence of markets where traveling merchants and dealers could meet.

As new professions came into being and people specialized more and more, social life became more complex. Religious practices were unified, and towns adopted their own personal gods. A ruling class of priests emerged who wielded authority, sometimes alone, sometimes alongside warrior chiefs and rich landowners.

The cities, attracting people and wealth like magnets, imposed their power over the surrounding countryside. To their religious, economic, and military authority was added the role of administration and government. Codes and laws were drawn up, defining everyone's duties, the division of labor, and the prices of goods. And all this made it necessary for people to invent a new means of communication — writing.

THE WALLS OF JERICHO

Near the modern town of Jericho, some 18 miles east of Jerusalem, lie the remains of the oldest town ever discovered. Buried nearly 65 feet deep under piles of earth and rock, its oldest houses go back to the eighth millennium B.C. Excavations show that at that time the site was peopled by hunters, fishermen, and farmers. These first occupants of Jericho lived in round mud-brick houses, protected by a defensive wall and a watchtower. As the centuries went by, the wall was reinforced, destroyed several times, and rebuilt. It was made of roughly hewn stone blocks put together without mortar. Houses were built against the walls and on the outside an enormous ditch about 25 feet wide and 10 feet deep was dug. Today, after 100 centuries of destruction and erosion, the remains of the ramparts are still up to 6 feet thick and stand nearly 13 feet high. This great wall is something of a mystery. Why did a prehistoric community with relatively few people to do the work build a wall of this size? Why did the population of Jericho, estimated to be 2,000 or 3,000 at the most, feel the need to protect itself in this way? The most likely explanation is that other people coveted the wealth of this town, which came in many forms.

One source of its wealth was water. Jericho was built close to a spring, which made it possible for the desert land to be transformed into a flourishing oasis. And from very early times the town had been at the junction of several busy highways, making it an active commercial center. In addition, Jericho lay very close to the Dead Sea, which provided an abundant supply of salt, a commodity that was particularly sought after for preserving food. Salt was exchanged for imported goods like obsidian, shellfish, iron ore, and turquoises.

THE SKULLS OF JERICHO

In 1953 some human skulls were discovered buried beneath one of the oldest walls of Jericho. The skulls had been covered with tinted plaster, and shells placed in their eye sockets. The plaster had been very carefully applied, modeled on the contours of the skulls so as to reproduce the dead person's features. Each model was completely individ- *ual, almost like a sculpted portrait. It is not known why this was done, but it may have been connected with an early form of ancestor worship. Possibly the survivors believed that by preserving their features, they could ensure that the spirits of the dead would continue to live.*

These five men, standing in the ruins of Jericho, mark the five different levels of the city, which go down 55 feet. The top man is at the surface of the site as it is today. The man below him is standing on the stone tower which overlooked the ramparts in 8000 B.C. The two below him are standing on the defensive wall of the same period, and the man at the bottom is on the edge of the ditch dug out of rock which protected the city.

The first inhabitants of Jericho built round houses using mud bricks made by hand and dried in the sun. A thousand years later the houses of Jericho had evolved and were square in shape. Some scholars believe that this transition from the round to the rectangular symbolizes a step forward in human evolution. Circular and semicircular patterns can be seen in nature in the shape of the planets, tree trunks, rainbows, and cave roofs. But the straight line and the right angle are generally constructions made by people.

Jericho and the Bible

The history of the city of Jericho has been preserved in the Bible in the Book of Joshua, which tells the story of its destruction by the Israelites. But this tale has not been confirmed by archaeological findings. In fact, it seems that at that time, around the eighth century B.C., Jericho was only a small collection of houses. However, its later days of splendor and its great walls were impressed in people's memory.

"Now Jericho was tightly shut because of the Israelites. No one went out and no one came in. Then the Lord said to Joshua, 'See, I have delivered Jericho into your hands, along with its king and its fighting men. March around the city once with all the armed men. Do this for six days. Have seven priests carry trumpets of rams' horns in front of the ark. On the seventh day, march around the city seven times with the priests blowing the trumpets. When you hear them sound a long blast on the trumpets, have all the people give a loud shout; then the wall of the city will collapse and the people will go up, every man straight in' . . . When the trumpets sounded, the people shouted, and at the sound of the trumpet, when the people gave a loud shout, the wall collapsed; so every man charged straight in, and they took the city. They devoted the city to the Lord and they destroyed with the sword every living thing in it—men and women, young and old, cattle, sheep, and donkeys."—Joshua 6: 1–21. The Holy Bible: New International Version. (Grand Rapids, MI, Zondervan, 1978).

ÇATAL HÜYÜK

In the sixth millennium B.C., the city of Çatal Hüyük in Anatolia covered over 38 acres and its population may have numbered as many as 6,000. The site was discovered by a group of English archaeologists in 1958. Under the direction of James Mellaart, they uncovered fourteen successive levels of houses, showing that for many centuries human beings had lived there continuously.

The first inhabitants of Çatal Hüyük were farmers. The town was built near a river which enabled the farmers to irrigate the land and get the most out of the soil. They grew two varieties of wheat, and barley, peas, and lentils. They may also have planted vineyards and orchards and begun to domesticate dogs and sheep. At that time, however, agriculture had not replaced fishing, wild-plant gathering, or above all, hunting: the region abounded in wild cattle, boars, deer, and leopards.

The varied and plentiful supply of food could support a large population, which in turn supplied enough labor to expand the cultivated land and develop animal husbandry, crafts, and trade and commerce with neighboring peoples. Deposits of obsidian located nearby also contributed to Çatal Hüyük's wealth. Obsidian is a translucent volcanic stone that is remarkably hard and durable. People used it to make not only tools, knife blades, and spear points but also mirrors and jewels. All these artifacts were used in trade with the rest of Asia Minor.

Technical and artistic know-how was not limited to obsidian working. The craftworkers of Çatal Hüyük were also highly skilled in the arts of pottery, basketmaking, wool weaving, and copper and lead working (from 6000 B.C.). Jewelers carved stones and shells, and artists decorated houses with wall paintings.

The economic and artistic importance of Çatal Hüyük extended to all the neighboring regions. But probably the most important cause of its unrivaled prestige was its role as a religious center.

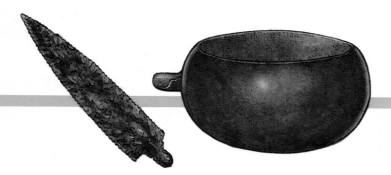

OBSIDIAN MIRRORS

Obsidian is a gray or black-looking volcanic stone. From prehistoric times it was highly valued and was used a great deal in trade. The main deposits were in Anatolia and Armenia. The people of those regions would barter obsidian for food or goods offered them by merchants, who often came from very far off. All over the Far East, archaeologists have found a multitude of objects worked in obsidian—daggers, ritual bowls, and highly polished fragments that were used as mirrors.

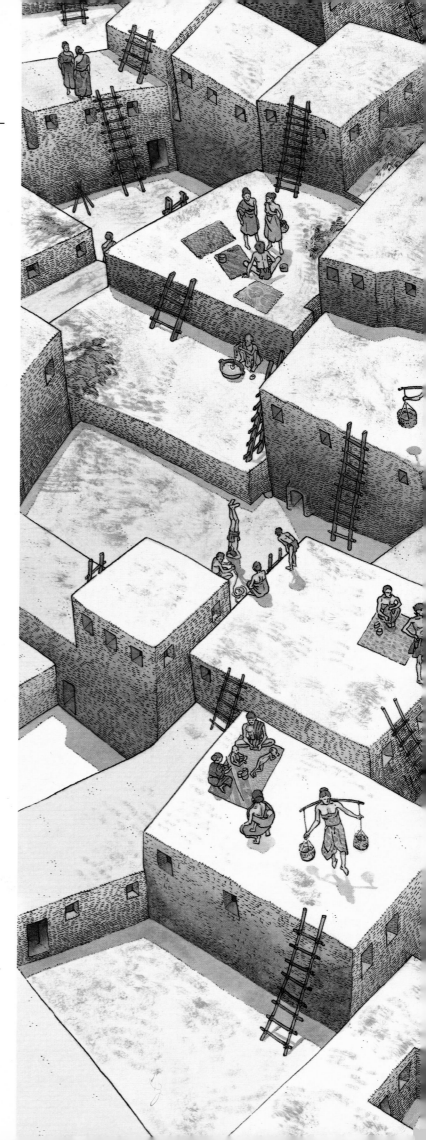

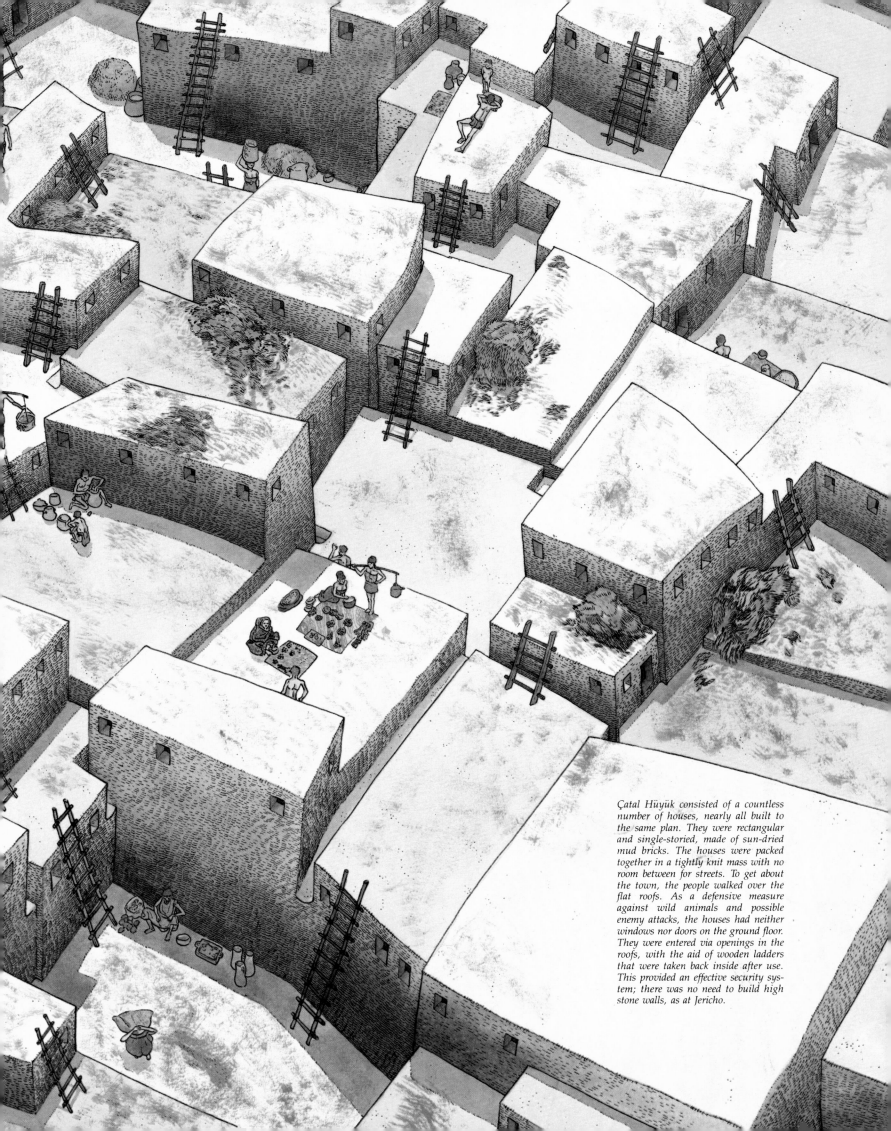

Çatal Hüyük consisted of a countless number of houses, nearly all built to the same plan. They were rectangular and single-storied, made of sun-dried mud bricks. The houses were packed together in a tightly knit mass with no room between for streets. To get about the town, the people walked over the flat roofs. As a defensive measure against wild animals and possible enemy attacks, the houses had neither windows nor doors on the ground floor. They were entered via openings in the roofs, with the aid of wooden ladders that were taken back inside after use. This provided an effective security system; there was no need to build high stone walls, as at Jericho.

THE VULTURE AND THE LEOPARD

The most remarkable feature of Çatal Hüyük is the importance that its people placed upon religion. Throughout the town the remains of a large number of shrines have been found. They are not large temples for worship, but ordinary buildings, only distinguishable from dwellings by their decorations and furnishings.

Among the wall paintings that have come to light, possibly the most extraordinary is one showing giant vultures circling above some decapitated human corpses. The meaning of this picture was made clear when several skeletons were found in houses and shrines, lying under plaster benches which served as seats and beds for the living.

Since no cemetery has been found, archaeologists have concluded that the dead were usually buried inside their own homes. For obvious reasons of hygiene, the bodies could not be allowed to decay inside the walls, so they would be carried outside the town, where vultures could be relied on to remove the flesh. The bodies were laid out on wooden or stone platforms built high enough to protect them from dogs and hyenas. Within a few days the vultures would have picked the bones clean. The rain, wind, and sun did the rest.

The skeletons were then carried back to Çatal Hüyük wrapped in woolen cloth or animal skins. Then they were partially or totally painted red and laid in their last resting place, under the benches upon which the living slept.

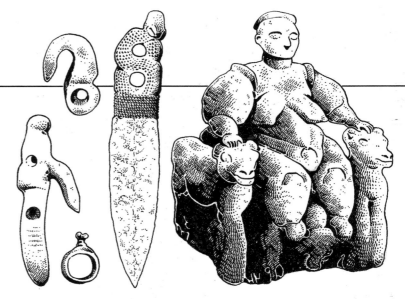

Bone rings and clothes fastenings. Flint daggers with hilts carved in the shape of coiled serpents.

This clay statuette, found in a Çatal Hüyük shrine, represents the mother goddess, her hands resting on the heads of two leopards. She is very fat and is giving birth to a child, who can be seen between her feet.

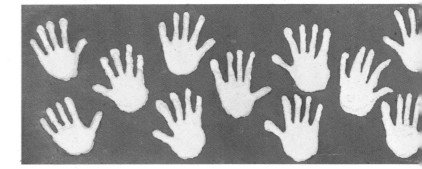

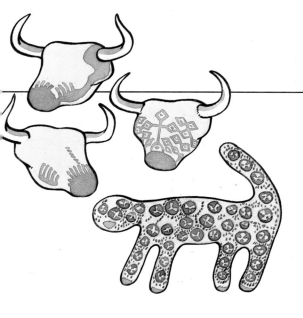

The houses and shrines of Çatal Hüyük are identical in plan. They are rectangular, with a central area covered with rushes and straw matting, and low benches all around the walls. The shrines often contain wall paintings of leopards, vultures, and bulls. Archaeologists have also found plaster reliefs of stylized leopards spotted with black and white rosettes, with splashes of red on their muzzles, paws, and tails. A quantity of groups of bulls' heads and wall paintings showing stylized vultures attacking headless human bodies have been found. Some shrines contain rows of hands painted simply by dipping a hand in watered down red clay and pressing it on the wall. This custom has continued for thousands of years in the nearby hamlet of Küçük Köy, where people still decorate their walls in this way.

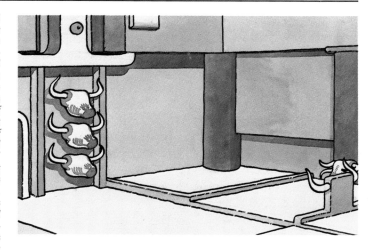

PEASANTS AND ARTISANS

The cultivation of cereals was started in the Near East. Several varieties of wheat and barley grew wild in this region. Around 8000 B.C. people stopped picking the plants as they found them and began trying to cultivate them. This brought about such an important change in the economy that the change is often referred to as the Neolithic Revolution, though it actually happened very slowly. The first farmers began by selecting the species that were the most nourishing and easiest to grow. By cultivating particular varieties, their successors produced cereal crops that were quick to ripen and whose grains steadily increased in size.

Around the same time, 6000 B.C., considerable advances were made in animal husbandry. Farmers learned to rear sheep and goats and a little later began domesticating cattle, pigs, and donkeys. Now, farmers had a constant supply of meat, milk, and wool, and valuable help in carrying loads. Moreover, all these developments encouraged craftworkers to improve their techniques, in basketwork for instance, and to develop new ones like weaving and pottery.

It was at Çatal Hüyük that the oldest pieces of fabric in the world were discovered—a few woven squares which have been dated from 6000 B.C.

Another change that had a vitally important effect on everyday life was the invention of pottery. For centuries the only known way of hardening clay was to dry it in the sun. Artifacts made in this way—usually dishes—cracked or broke at the slightest knock. In the Near East, around 6500 B.C., a method of firing clay was invented that made it possible for pottery to be manufactured and used much more widely.

Although still primitive, some beautiful things were made using this technique. But it was not until the invention of the potter's wheel, around 3500 B.C., that potters began making much finer artifacts.

THE FIRST FABRICS

The oldest fabrics in the world come from the shrouds in which the people of Çatal Hüyük wrapped the bones of their dead. Experts who have analyzed the fabrics have established that great care went into preparing the fibers before spinning them and into the weaving itself. Unfortunately, the pieces of fabric were carbonized when found. Despite chemical tests and analyses under microscopes, the kinds of fibers used remains a mystery. They may be of vegetable origin, like linen, or of animal origin, like wool. The colors and designs have also been lost, but we can guess what they looked like from the wall decorations discovered at Çatal Hüyük.

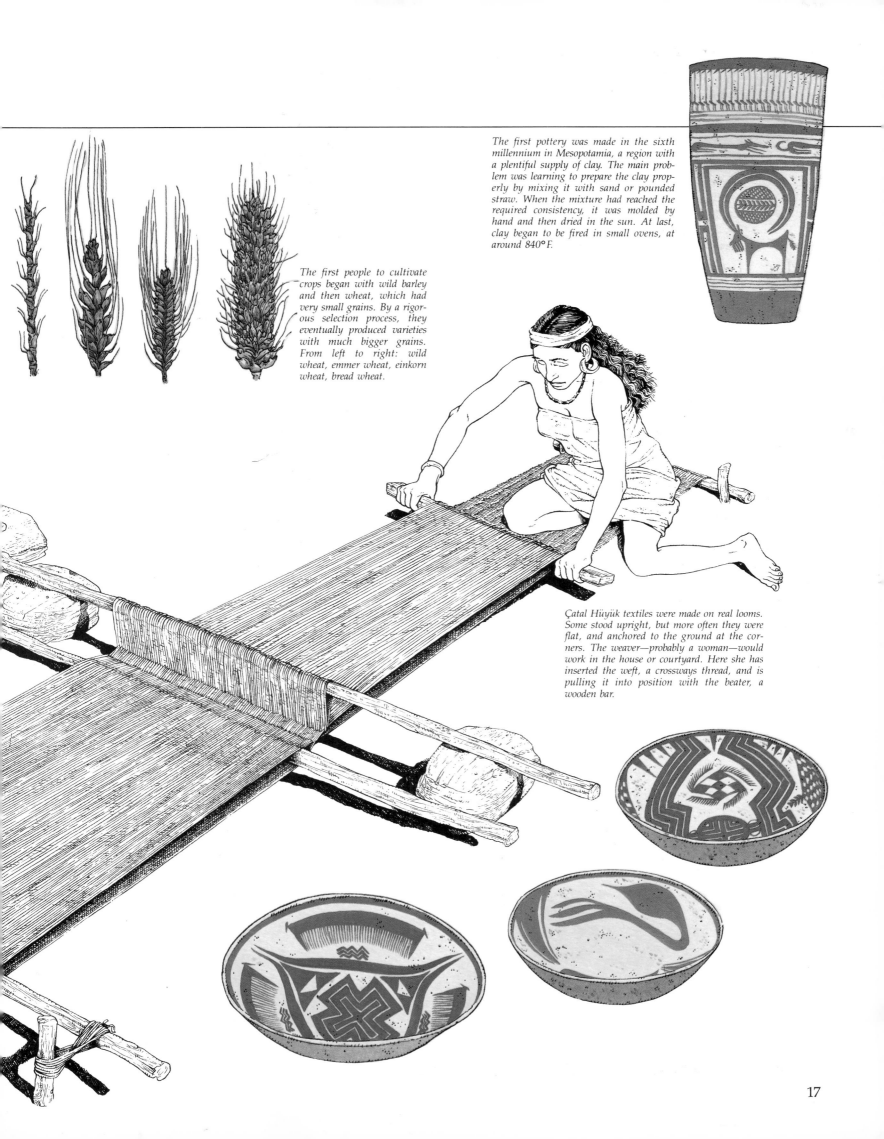

The first pottery was made in the sixth millennium in Mesopotamia, a region with a plentiful supply of clay. The main problem was learning to prepare the clay properly by mixing it with sand or pounded straw. When the mixture had reached the required consistency, it was molded by hand and then dried in the sun. At last, clay began to be fired in small ovens, at around 840° F.

The first people to cultivate crops began with wild barley and then wheat, which had very small grains. By a rigorous selection process, they eventually produced varieties with much bigger grains. From left to right: wild wheat, emmer wheat, einkorn wheat, bread wheat.

Çatal Hüyük textiles were made on real looms. Some stood upright, but more often they were flat, and anchored to the ground at the corners. The weaver—probably a woman—would work in the house or courtyard. Here she has inserted the weft, a crossways thread, and is pulling it into position with the beater, a wooden bar.

MESOPOTAMIA

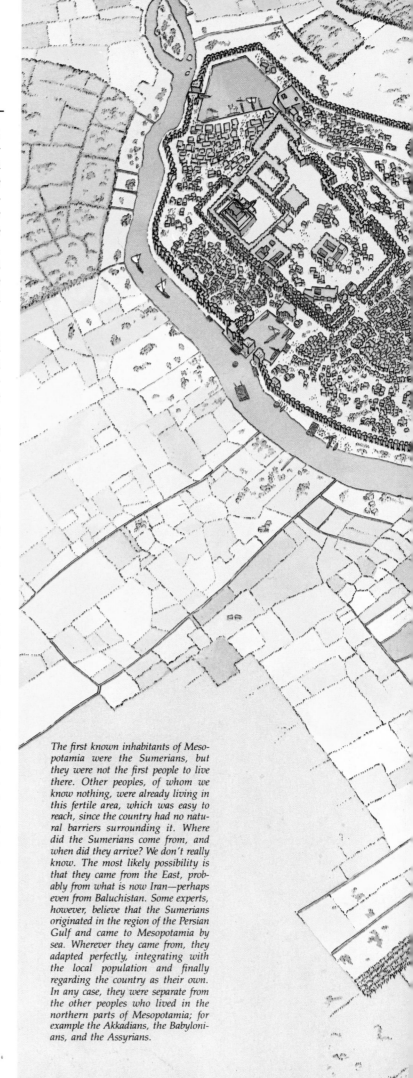

The name *Mesopotamia* comes from the Greek, meaning "the land between two rivers." It was given by a historian of antiquity, Polybius, to the Near Eastern region embraced by the Tigris on the east and the Euphrates on the west. These two great rivers rise near each other in the mountains of Armenia and run parallel for about 600 miles; then they join up to form what is now called the Shatt-al-Arab before pouring into the waters of the Persian Gulf. In the north, Mesopotamia is a land of plateaus; in the south it consists of a huge unbroken plain. It was in this vast region that one of the most brilliant civilizations the world has ever known flourished for nearly 3,000 years.

It is difficult to get a real idea of this ancient land today, now that it is a near desert, its soil rendered sterile by salt and burned dry by the sun. But 5,000 years ago it was possible for a balance to exist here between people and their natural environment; a harmonious combination of water, earth, and heat made this area immensely rich.

The Greek historian Herodotus described Egypt as "a gift from the Nile." It could equally well be said that Mesopotamia was a gift from the twin rivers, the Tigris and the Euphrates. The annual melting of the snow in the mountains where they began caused them to flood violently every year. Their waters poured onto the plain at the season when the sun was at its hottest, with the temperature rarely falling below 100° F. Water is essential to life, and farmers need to develop means of controlling any excesses or lacks of it. In contrast with the very regular annual flooding of the Nile from the great African lakes, the flooding of the Tigris and the Euphrates was unpredictable, depending on how much rain or snow had fallen in the Armenian mountains. Their waters filled the plain between April and June, too soon for a summer harvest and too late for a winter one. So it fell to the farmers to provide the soil with only as much water as it needed; fields had to be irrigated, not drowned.

The first great art of the Mesopotamians was to control the rivers. Wherever they could they built artificial dikes, dug reservoirs and drainage ditches, and organized collective irrigation systems. And the fertilized soil repaid them by providing magnificent harvests—sometimes even two harvests a year—which were the envy of the ancient world. In the oases these farmers created, millions of palm trees provided cool shade.

Under the burning Mesopotamian sun and despite the salt that was a constant threat to the fertility of the soil in the lower parts of the plain, an intensive system of agriculture was developed, providing the people with both food and wealth.

The first known inhabitants of Mesopotamia were the Sumerians, but they were not the first people to live there. Other peoples, of whom we know nothing, were already living in this fertile area, which was easy to reach, since the country had no natural barriers surrounding it. Where did the Sumerians come from, and when did they arrive? We don't really know. The most likely possibility is that they came from the East, probably from what is now Iran—perhaps even from Baluchistan. Some experts, however, believe that the Sumerians originated in the region of the Persian Gulf and came to Mesopotamia by sea. Wherever they came from, they adapted perfectly, integrating with the local population and finally regarding the country as their own. In any case, they were separate from the other peoples who lived in the northern parts of Mesopotamia; for example the Akkadians, the Babylonians, and the Assyrians.

Cylinder seal of the scribe Zagganita, around 2250 B.C., showing the gods gathering in triumphant celebration of the renewal of nature in spring. Cylinder seals were small stone tubes with designs carved into them; the design could be impressed in wet clay by rolling the seal over it.

THE FLOOD

One day the Lord became angry with the human race; although it was still in its infancy, he denounced it as weak and corrupt. As a punishment, he created a great deluge to purify the earth and wipe out every living thing . . . with the exception of one just man, who was to father a new breed of humanity. Thus goes the story of the Flood.

This myth is one of the oldest known to us. It is told in a number of different cultures, though the Biblical version in the Book of Genesis is by far the most widely known. This tells how Jahweh instructed Noah to build an ark to protect his family, together with one male and one female of every living creature, for the forty days during which "the windows of the heavens were opened" and "all the fountains of the great deep were broken up." But the Hebrews did not invent this myth. They probably borrowed it from the Babylonians, who themselves had adapted even older versions told by the Sumerians and the Akkadians.

In 1872 a young English orientalist, George Smith, found some fragments of Sumerian tablets, which he was able to identify, piece together, and translate. His research, together with some more recent discoveries, has made it possible to reconstruct the oldest version of the Flood myth.

The Sumerian text sets the story in the five great royal cities of Mesopotamia—Eridu, Bad-Tibira, Larak, Sippar, and Shuruppak. The wickedness of their inhabitants aroused the wrath of the gods, particularly of the supreme god, Enlil, who decided to wipe out humanity with a great flood. Nothing would change his mind, neither the prayers of Inanna, goddess of love and war, nor those of Enki, protector of humankind. Since he was unable to save the whole of humanity from the threatened punishment, Enki decided to preserve one man, Ziusudra, king of Shuruppak, who feared and revered the gods. Warned of the impending disaster by the kindly Enki, Ziusudra set about building a big boat in which he and his family could survive with a number of animals. Then torrential rains beat down on the earth. For six days and six nights, the winds were unleashed, sweeping all from their path. The waters rose and covered the earth, swallowing up every living thing. The darkened world was lit only by flashes of lightning tearing through the sky. Finally the storm ended. Ziusudra waited six more days and then set a dove free; it could find nowhere to perch and came back. Next he sent out a swallow, which also returned. Finally, Ziusudra let loose a raven, which did not come back. Knowing that he could now disembark, Ziusudra offered a sacrifice to the gods, who were astonished to discover that the human race had not been completely destroyed. The terrible Enlil was appeased and forgave human beings, who were now allowed to repopulate the earth. As for Ziusudra, the gods carried him away to the faraway land "at the mouths of the rivers," where he lived forever.

Mount Ararat rises in the north of what is now Turkey; its main peak is 16,916 feet high. This is where, according to the Bible, Noah's ark landed. "But God remembered Noah and all the wild animals and the livestock that were with him in the ark, and he sent a wind over the earth and the waters receded. Now the springs of the deep and the floodgates of the heavens had been closed, and the rain had stopped falling from the sky. The water receded steadily from the earth. At the end of the hundred and fifty days the water had gone down, and on the seventeenth day of the seventh month the ark came to rest on the mountains of Ararat . . . After forty days Noah opened the window he had made in the ark and sent out a raven, and it kept flying back and forth until the water had dried up from the earth."—Genesis 8:1–7. The Holy Bible: New International Version. (Grand Rapids, MI, Zondervan, 1978).

There is a lot of evidence to suggest that for the Sumerians and Babylonians the Flood was more than a myth—that it was a real, historical event. The Sumerian "royal list" found at Nippur states that after several thousand years (241,200, to be exact) the "Flood leveled everything" and nothing was as it had been before. Archaeologists have looked for evidence of this cataclysm to place and date it. To date, three Mesopotamian cities—Ur, Kish, and Shuruppak—have yielded deep sedimentary deposits of fluvial origin, indicating that a very big flood could have taken place. Discoveries like this support the theory that there was a real flood—in that area, at least. One of the deposits, at Ur, goes down nearly 13 feet! But at Eridu, only seven miles away, digging down to levels below any human remains has not shown the slightest traces of flooding. So the mystery of the Flood is far from solved and will surely continue to inspire curiosity and fascination.

URUK

Jericho and Çatal Hüyük were the earliest examples of urban civilizations. During the centuries that followed, a dozen much larger cities rose up between the Tigris and the Euphrates. Each had power over a huge agricultural area and several villages. Each, in fact, amounted to a small state with its own laws, customs, and gods. Uruk, now called Warka, on the banks of the Euphrates, was the oldest of these city-states in the land of Sumer. Between 3500 and 3000 B.C., Uruk won a position through warfare and conflict as the most powerful and best organized of all the neighboring rival cities.

Excavations at Uruk have uncovered eighteen successive levels of occupation. In these layers, archaeologists can read the long history of the city's progress from a small farming settlement to a prosperous town with forty thousand inhabitants.

The earliest levels show that the development of the town crystallized around the temples. In the middle of the fourth millennium, the agricultural system was rigorously organized; to increase production and reduce the threat of famine, many dikes, irrigation channels, and reservoirs were built. In charge of the work were the priests, who supervised the continued upkeep of the system, with the help of a large rural labor force.

Thus the city ensured its domination over a vast territory that could supply the needs of a population that was growing daily. The activities of these people revolved around the life of the temple. Some, of course, were priests, but there were also scribes, architects, overseers, soldiers, administrators, and craftworkers.

Uruk covered 1,000 acres; it had grown up out of two neighboring settlements, Eanna to the east and Kullaba to the west. The city retained traces of its dual origins: one sector was dedicated to An, the sky god, and the other to Inanna, goddess of love and fertility (who became Ishtar under the Babylonians). In honor of these powerful, awe-inspiring but beneficent beings, the people of Uruk built magnificent temples.

The section of the city consecrated to the goddess contained at least four monumental temples as well as a stepped tower (ziggurat). One of these temples (called the Limestone Temple), standing on a foundation of stone, measured 260 feet long and 100 feet wide. The section of the city devoted to the high god Anu was especially remarkable for the artificial hill on which his temple was raised. The hill was more than 40 feet high and on top was constructed a small white temple, undoubtedly the earthly residence of the god. In raising the sanctuary toward the heavens, the faithful wanted to facilitate the descent of the god to the city. By living among men, he would be able to give them his favors: peace, the mercy of heaven, and an abundant harvest.

THE "LADY OF WARKA"

This marble portrait of a woman found at Uruk is one of the masterpieces of ancient art. The eyes and eyebrows were inlaid with shells and colored stones. Although the shells and stones have now vanished, the face still has extraordinary power and character.

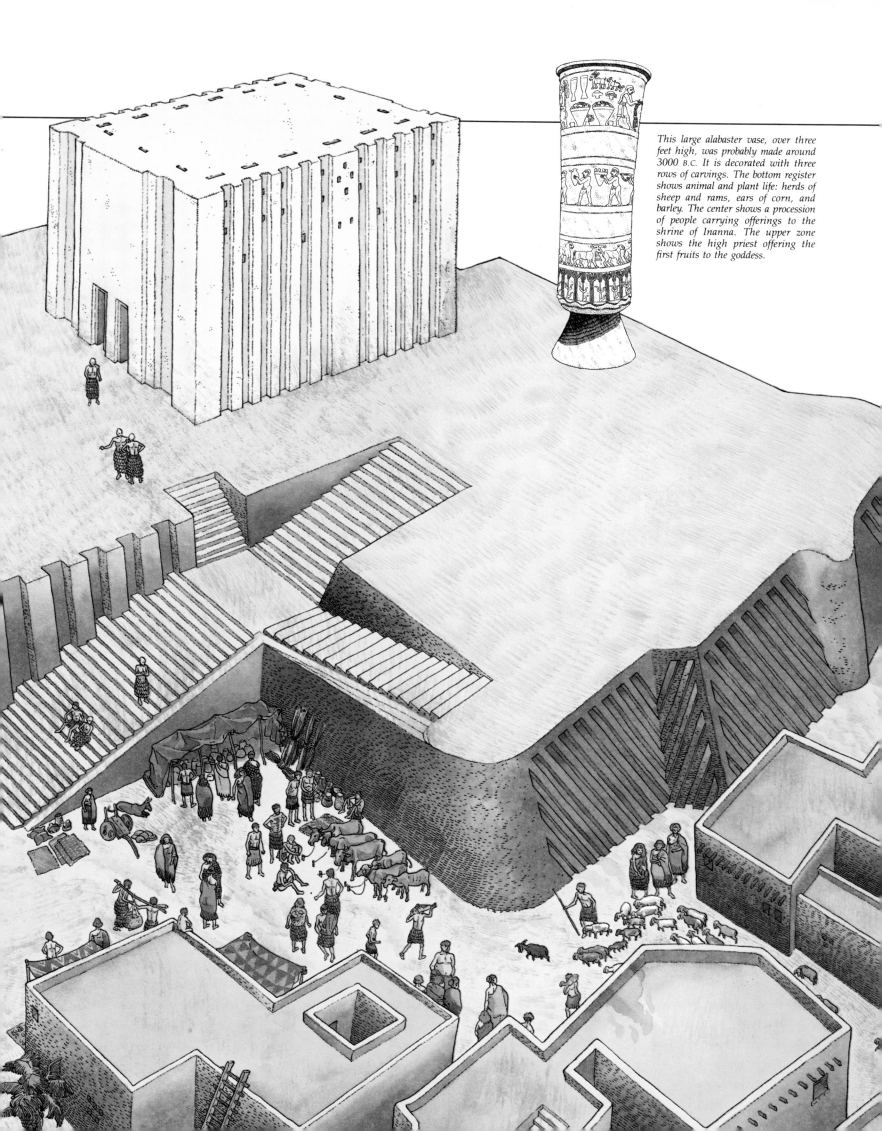

This large alabaster vase, over three feet high, was probably made around 3000 B.C. It is decorated with three rows of carvings. The bottom register shows animal and plant life: herds of sheep and rams, ears of corn, and barley. The center shows a procession of people carrying offerings to the shrine of Inanna. The upper zone shows the high priest offering the first fruits to the goddess.

THE PEOPLE AND THEIR GODS

In Mesopotamia, people's religious beliefs were completely woven into their daily lives. Everyone from king to slave believed that their existence on earth depended on the will of the gods, whom they had to serve and worship. The king was the chief among the faithful, and Sumerian mythology constantly reminded him that he held his power only as long as the god who protected his city willed it.

If the protector god was angered or annoyed, he could heap misfortunes on the person of the king and on his subjects; if pleased, he could shower them with blessings. The people's first duty was to pray and to take offerings to the great temples. The archives of Uruk tell us that the daily menu required by the four chief gods of the city consisted of 250 loaves, over 1,000 date tartlets, 50 sheep, 8 lambs, 2 oxen, and 1 calf. All these provisions would first be presented to the statues of the gods; then they went to feed the priests and all the people who worked for the temple—fishermen, shepherds, craftworkers, scribes, and builders; anything left over was given to beggars and the poor. A clay tablet found at Lagash and dating from 3000 B.C. gives a list of the rations handed out every day: bread, meat, and beer were distributed to twelve hundred men and women.

As well as offerings and sacrifices, the gods demanded that people lead a blameless life, cultivating virtues such as filial love, honesty, and respect for the laws and the established order. In return, the gods granted the people aid and protection and promised a happy future in the life beyond. Thousands of tombs filled with funeral goods attest to a universal belief in an afterlife. For the Sumerians it was a sacred duty to bury the dead and honor them. Should they neglect to do so, the ghost of the dead person would wander on earth forever and torment the living.

A WORSHIPER FROM ESHNUNNA

Portraits like this were deliberately unrealistic, in an effort to portray the mystical ecstasy of a man at prayer. The enormous eyes and dilated pupils suggest that the worshiper has been transfixed by a vision of the divinity. This statuette, 29 inches high, was made at the beginning of the third millennium B.C. It was found at Eshnunna, in the temple of the god Abu.

In all the Sumerian cities, the temples occupied a vast space in the center of a sacred area, usually dominated by a broad stepped tower called a ziggurat. At the summit stood a shrine dedicated to one or several gods. Ziggurats were built on square bases with sides 140 to 120 feet long, and some were over 65 feet high. The farmers working 12 miles away on the plain had only to lift their eyes to see the house of their god and master. A fantastic amount of work went into buildings like this. It has now been calculated that the base alone of the Ziggurat of Uruk would have taken fifteen hundred men five years to build.

Among the most important religious ceremonies of Sumer were the banquets of the gods. Several times a year the priests would gather together a small group of worshipers in the country, on river boats, or, most often, within the temple precincts. Men and women carrying ritual goblets would go to the temple, where they were welcomed by the priests. They were admitted to the presence of the god and invited to join in the celebration.

Around 3500 B.C. the Mesopotamian pantheon included several dozen gods, each with a specific role.

An (or **Anu**) was the most powerful, as father and lord of the gods. He was represented by the sky. The center of his worship was at Uruk.

Enlil gradually supplanted **An** as the chief god. He was lord of the breath and ruled over air and earth; his city was Nippur.

Enki was lord of fresh waters and of the underground world. He was god of wisdom, and also the friend of humans. During the flourishing of the Babylonian culture he became the father of **Marduk**, god of Babylon. His city was Eridu.

Nannar (or **Sin**) was the moon god. He presided over the city of Ur.

Utu (**Shamash** in Babylonia) was the god of justice and truth. His symbol was the sun. He was worshiped at Larsa.

Inanna (**Ishtar** in Babylon) was the greatest of the goddesses. She reigned over heaven and earth. She brought love to people, but she also brought war. She became the **Astarte** of the Phoenicians, the **Aphrodite** of the Greeks, and the **Venus** of the Romans. Her city was Uruk.

25

BUILDING A TEMPLE

To build their houses and, more importantly, large buildings like temples and palaces, the Sumerians had to overcome a serious difficulty. There was absolutely no source of building stone in the country, and the only available wood was palm, which was too fibrous for building. However, the builders did have an endless supply of one material that cost virtually nothing—clay mud. They used it to make bricks, mixing earth with chopped straw, stirring in water, and pouring the mixture into molds. It only took a few hours for the bricks to dry and harden in the scorching Mesopotamian sun. When the Sumerians wanted to put up buildings that would last longer than ordinary houses, the bricks were fired in a kiln and covered with bitumen as they were laid. Whether dried or fired, these bricks provided a building material that was quite strong but not very attractive. So the architects took pains to brighten up the buildings by decorating them, whitewashing the exterior walls and putting statues in the temples, which were probably very dark inside.

Every king wanted to glorify his reign by building a great temple in the heart of his city; hundreds of slaves would be assigned to the task, as would a large proportion of war booty. Gudea, king of Lagash in the twenty-first century B.C., devoted his reign to building and restoring temples; a statue of him has been found with an architectural plan laid on his knees. In pursuit of his aims, he had rare and expensive materials brought from far away: cedarwood for the framework and ebony for the decor; hard stones like diorite and steatite for the carvings and statues; gold, copper, and carnelian to make the finest jewels. Centuries later, unfortunately, little remains of all this splendor. Most of the monuments have crumbled and fallen, forming small mounds called *tells*, which can still be seen today on the Mesopotamian plain.

Ur-Nanshe, king of Lagash around 2540 B.C., had his work commemorated on this stone plaque. He is shown above on the left carrying on his head a basket of building clay to symbolize the construction of a new temple. Below on the right, the work is complete and he and his son celebrate the founding of the sanctuary.

Gudea with the flowing jar
This diorite statue, 25 inches high, is in the Louvre Museum in Paris. The waters of fertility gushing from the jar commemorate Gudea's benevolence toward his kingdom. The cuneiform inscription reads as follows: "To Geshtinanna, his lady, Gudea, prince of Lagash, his temple of Girsu has built, her own statue he made which he named 'Geshtinanna bestows life' and he placed it in the temple of the goddess."

The mosaics of Uruk
Cone mosaics were invented by the architects of Uruk to decorate their plain mudbrick sanctuaries. They covered the walls and pillars with a tapestry of multicolored geometric designs by setting different-colored conical studs of fired clay into the fresh plaster.

THE LEGEND OF GILGAMESH

The tale of the fabulous adventures of the hero Gilgamesh was for the Mesopotamians what the *Iliad* and the *Odyssey* were for the Greeks. It was an epic poem based on a historical person and enriched with a number of supernatural events. It served both to teach and to inspire pride in the whole nation.

Gilgamesh was the son of a minor god and a human mother. He became the fifth king of Uruk and was a very oppressive ruler. He forced the people to superhuman labors building the walls of the city and exercised his rights over the young maidens of the land. The people complained to the gods and were heard. The city god Anu had an animal-man of extraordinary strength created to stand up to Gilgamesh; his name was Enkidu. But Enkidu, whose body was covered with hair, and who had no knowledge of civilization, living and grazing with the wild beasts, now became completely transformed. A woman of Uruk seduced him and taught him to love; after this, he became Gilgamesh's inseparable friend. The two companions felt so strong together that they left Uruk to accomplish brave deeds and fulfill their destiny as superheroes.

They set off for the distant Forest of Cedars, which was guarded by the giant Humbaba. They decided to challenge him by cutting down his fine cedars, one by one. Humbaba was enraged, and his weapons were terrible: his mouth spat fire and his breath alone could kill. But the heroes pierced him with their swords, cut off his head, and returned to Uruk in triumph.

Emboldened by his victory, Gilgamesh defied Ishtar, one of the city goddesses. Furious, she let loose the Bull of Heaven to ravage Uruk and kill Gilgamesh. The monster swiftly turned fields to desert, dried up the rivers, and with his breath opened crevasses in the earth that swallowed up hundreds of citizens. The two heroes arrived at the height of the massacre. Enkidu seized the bull's horns while Gilgamesh struck it with his sword, tore out its heart, and threw one of its thighs in Ishtar's face.

The gods could stand no more! They inflicted a sickness on Enkidu; after seven days of agony, he died in his friend's arms. Now alone and afraid of death, Gilgamesh tried to escape his human destiny. He set off in search of the supreme secret, the secret of eternal life. Only one person could reveal it to him, Ziusudra, to whom the gods had granted immortality after he survived the Flood.

After a long quest, Gilgamesh found the old man, who told him where he could find the "Plant of Life," which would ward off death forever: it was growing at the bottom of the ocean. Undaunted, Gilgamesh tied some heavy stones to his feet, dived into the sea, and picked the plant. He started on his homeward journey, anxious to share his prize with the people of Uruk, Alas! While he was swimming, a serpent snatched the miraculous plant and made off with it. Neither Gilgamesh nor humanity would have eternal life.

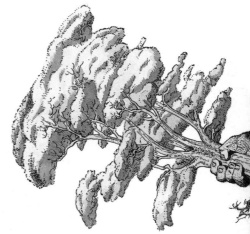

Gilgamesh with a lion
This colossal gypsum statue, 16 feet high, is in the Louvre Museum in Paris. It comes from the royal palace of Sargon II (721 B.C.–705 B.C.) at Khorsabad in Iraq, where it guarded a doorway.

The Epic of Gilgamesh *was known throughout all Mesopotamia and beyond, and it inspired a great number of works of art. Hundreds of cylinder seals representing episodes from the hero's life have survived to the present day.*

The oldest written records seem to indicate that Gilgamesh was a real person in Sumerian history. He is described as the fifth king of the first dynasty of Uruk, reigning in the middle of the third millennium. Until then, Uruk had been separated by a river from its neighbor, Koulaba. Gilgamesh organized a huge building program to divert the course of the river and surrounded the two cities with a wall six miles long with nine hundred watchtowers.
Through this gigantic achievement the king and his reign were immortalized. Shortly after his death, Gilgamesh became a hero. Poets sang of his deeds and every year the list of his exploits grew longer. At the beginning of the second millennium, the epic reached its final form. We have almost all of it, in twelve tablets containing over thirty-five hundred verses. They were discovered at Nineveh during the excavation of the library of the Assyrian king Ashurbanipal.

ALL-POWERFUL MONARCHS

At the time of the earliest Sumerian dynasties (up to 3000 B.C.), the king was given the title *En*, which can be translated as "Lord." He was the custodian of civil and religious power, exercising total authority over his subjects. The palace and temple were one, with the king acting as the earthly representative of the city's presiding god. Around 2700 B.C., in the town of Kish, the first royal palace was built that was independent of the temple, an unmistakable sign that the monarchy had been separated from the priesthood. After this date, the king's title En, was replaced by *Lugal*, meaning "King" or "Great Man."

As the centuries went by, the king's authority was consolidated. There was more peace between the cities, which had formerly risen up against each other in rivalry, and the clash of arms was heard less often. True dynasties were founded, giving greater stability to the heads of state. Monarchies became hereditary, normally passing from father to son. The king's wife certainly had a public role, but she never reigned alone. The archives only mention one woman who ruled as sovereign for a few years over the city of Kish.

The king had control of political and economic power, and to some degree, religious power as well. He was certainly the richest man in his kingdom, his wealth coming from booty won at war and taxes paid by his subjects. He was a great landlord, often owning thousands of acres of farmland. He was assisted by an efficient and stable administration, and he surrounded himself with civil servants whose loyalty he assured by paying them well, usually in the form of landed property.

SARGON OF AKKAD

After 2400 B.C. the Sumerian cities gave up quarreling with each other to face some hugely ambitious rivals, the Akkadians, Semitic people from the north. One of them, Sargon of Akkad, also called Sargon the Great, was a key personality in Mesopotamian history. His reign marks the decline of the city-states and the founding of a true empire. He made such a powerful impression on his contemporaries that his reign became a legend. He is described as an invincible conqueror who subjected the adjacent kingdoms one after the other and controlled an enormous empire.

How the king spent his time
As supreme commander of the armies, the king himself led his troops into battle in times of war. In peacetime he managed day-to-day affairs with the support of efficient advisors. He also busied himself with the digging and upkeep of the canals, which were essential to the life and wealth of the kingdom. But the first duty of the Mesopotamian king was above all the building, maintenance, and decoration of the city temples.

THE "DEATH PIT"

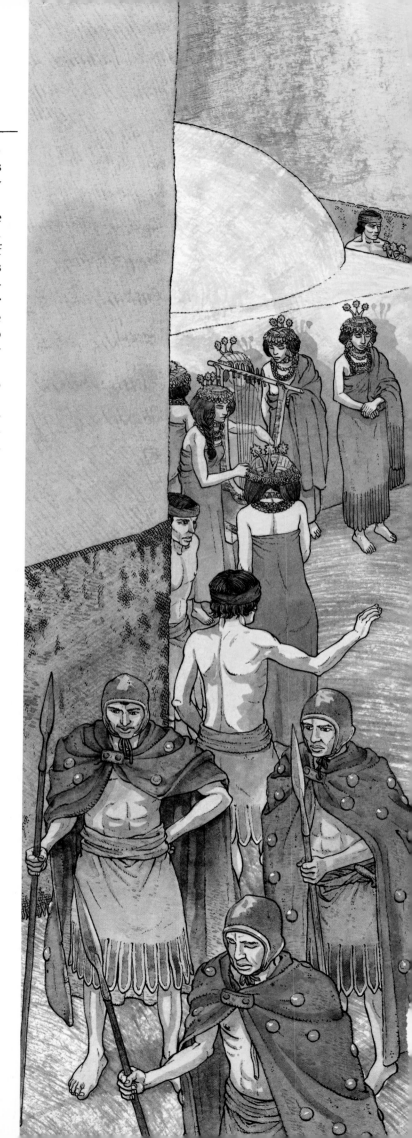

I t is late afternoon in Ur, and the narrow streets, usually so crowded and noisy, are nearly empty. The Euphrates is empty of shipping traffic and the harbor district, usually filled with a motley crowd, looks fast asleep.

Since early morning, people have been crowding into the temple precincts to attend the funeral of their queen Puabi, who died yesterday. A muffled sound announces the arrival of the funeral procession, which at last comes into view. At its head, soldiers march with solemn steps, their faces expressionless. On their heads they wear heavy copper helmets, and their bodies are swathed in long capes. They march in time to the regular beat of big skin drums struck by the musicians who come after them. Other musicians pluck the strings of richly ornamented harps while priestesses utter cries of mourning. The body of the dead queen lies on a chariot drawn by two wild asses. So that her people can see her on her last voyage, she has not been wrapped in a shroud, but laid on a coffin. Her face is pale against the glittering frame of her magnificient headdress, from which gold leaf and gold rings cascade over her closed eyes. At her throat and wrists gleam jewels of gold, emerald, and lapis lazuli. Behind the funeral chariot walks a procession of servants holding the treasures the queen is to take with her into the afterlife—precious dishes, rare shells, statuettes, and jewels. They are followed by some twenty court ladies, most of them very young, dressed in long red or blue dresses and wearing rich headdresses and bright jewelry. The attentive crowd looks for signs of pallor beneath their heavy makeup, and their eyes, gazing fixedly into the distance, seem curiously blank. The procession stops at the entrance to the tomb. Some temple servants bring forward an ox and a goat and the high priest performs the sacrifice, slitting the animals' throats over a stone slab. The rites complete, the procession continues down the gently sloping ramp, which leads to the royal tomb several feet underground. To the sound of funereal chanting, four soldiers carry Puabi's litter along the underground passage into a cavern scented by burning incense. In the antechamber and passage, the court ladies, servants, soldiers, and even the animals who accompanied the procession take their places. Standing stock still, they wait, falling silent as the songs of the musicians mingle with the faint sounds of life outside.

Suddenly, the little daylight penetrating the underground chamber disappears. The entrance to the tomb above has been blocked by stone and earth.

By the light of oil lamps, each person present approaches a large jar, dips a cup into it and swallows the contents in one gulp. The animals, too, are given poison. The poison takes effect within a few minutes: the bulls grow feeble as their lifeblood drains away; the last strains of harp music die away and voices fade in a last sigh.

Forty-five centuries ago in the city of Ur, fifty-three men and women sacrificed their lives so that they could go on serving their sovereign in the kingdom of shadows.

The royal tombs of Ur were found in 1926 by the English archaeologist Sir Charles Leonard Woolley. For several months he and his team had been digging in the area around the temple, looking for tombs. Their hopes were fulfilled beyond their wildest dreams when, after digging a very deep trench, they reached the "death pit." In the faint light entering it for the first time in 45 centuries, they saw dozens of skeletons surrounded by gold and silver, lying as on the day of their death. Their last home, ignored by tomb robbers, had barely been touched by the passage of time.

BURIED TREASURE

The discovery of the royal tombs of Ur was a wonderful find for archaeologists. It revealed hitherto unknown funeral practices, not mentioned in the written texts, and the artifacts placed alongside the dead provided evidence of the high quality attained by Sumerian craftsmanship.

The gold objects found in the "death pit" are unique masterpieces. They probably represent the most elaborate workmanship of the day: a precious material like gold was only entrusted to the most skilled craftworkers. Since gold does not deteriorate, these artifacts were found, despite their long burial underground, in exactly the same condition as when they left the hands of their creators nearly 5,000 years ago. The goldsmith's skills were already fully developed: techniques such as cloisonné (enamel), filigree, and chasing, and soldering gold held no secrets for him.

The pieces of jewelry also attest to the amazing prosperity of Ur in the middle of the third millenium, and the vitality of its foreign trade. None of the materials used could be found in Sumer; they had to be imported, sometimes from very far away. Gold, first of all, was used widely for plates and dishes, ceremonial weapons, and all kinds of ornaments; there were other metals, too, such as copper and silver, and semiprecious stones like lapis lazuli, turquoise, and carnelian, all of which had to be imported, mainly from Eastern countries. Then there were seashells and mother-of-pearl, possibly from Dilmun, a place described in legend which may have been one of the Bahrain Islands in the Persian Gulf.

These buried treasures attracted numbers of pillagers from the time of antiquity onward, they looted the tombs and removed their most valuable contents. Sometimes the remains of tunnels can be found on the sites of royal tombs, built by robbers to gain access to the loot. So often, archaeologists have had to be content with a few scattered fragments, a golden diadem here, a few valueless copper pots there, or silver pieces which the robbers have left behind in favor of masterpieces of gold and precious stones.

A court musician playing one of the harps found in the royal tombs of Ur. The outstanding decorative feature is the splendid bull's head in gold, in which are inlaid large lapis lazuli eyes. Its expressive character is accentuated by its upward-pointing horns and curious lapis lazuli beard.

It is believed that when the harp was played, the sound resembled the lowing of a bull. The sound box is decorated with a mosaic of shells and red and blue stones. On the uprights, similar mosaic patterns alternate with bands of gold leaf. The rest of the harp, which was probably in wood, has not survived its long stay underground.

GOLDEN DAGGERS

Like the other daggers found in the royal tombs, this weapon is for show and would not have been used for fighting. The hilt is carved from a single block of lapis lazuli of exceptional color and quality and decorated with gold studs arranged in triangles. On the smooth gold blade is a short inscription. The sheath is a masterpiece of workmanship. Its base is covered with a rich filigree decoration imitating the sheaths of plaited straw used for ordinary daggers, and over this is a fine network of gold.

A court lady wearing some of the jewels found on several female skeletons in the royal tombs. The headdress is the most spectacular item. It is based on a kind of hairnet of ribbons on which several rows of colored stones are fastened to form a coronet; from this, small gold rings and a fringe of gold beech leaves hang over the brow. Then, fixed to the back of the head and rising above it is an ornament composed of three eight-petaled flowers in gold. As well as wearing diadems, several of the court ladies wore huge earrings in the form of cornucopias. The earrings were so heavy that they had to be attached to the wearer's hair as well as to her ears.

A prince or court dignitary of Ur, carrying the ceremonial weapons found in the tombs. The golden helmet must have been worn on state occasions only, certainly not during battle; gold is far too soft to protect the head during a fight! The helmet is made from a single gold sheet shaped and finely chased to look like a wig. The ears are in relief, and fine lines represent hair. The helmet was laced to a quilted lining through the small holes pierced around the edges.

THE FABULOUS CITY OF MARI

The site of Mari (now Tell Hariri in Syria) was discovered quite by accident one August day in 1933. Some peasants who were looking for some large stones to put on a relative's tomb discovered a very ancient-looking statue in the sand. Excavations were begun at once, and a team of French archaeologists, led by André Parrot, uncovered the remains of an entire city. Mari, one of the capitals of ancient Mesopotamia, rose from the sands once more.

Before excavation it was known that the city had existed, but no one had any idea of its size. A few cuneiform tablets listed the dynasties that had ruled over it. The archives of Hammurabi, king of Babylon in the eighteenth century B.C., record the defeat and destruction of Mari, and how its walls were leveled to the ground.

Today, 50 years of careful excavation have given us a complete knowledge of the city. Some splendid architectural finds have been unearthed—houses, temples, and palaces, statues of all sizes, wall paintings, and jewelry. Finally, over twenty thousand inscribed tablets, stored in the palace archive room, have made it possible to reconstruct the history of the Mesopotamian world in the third and second millennia B.C.

As a result of all this, we now know that Mari was one of the largest Eastern capitals of antiquity. It was a political and religious center of the first order, and the home of an unrivaled artistic culture. The city's splendor also derived from its commercial activities. Foreign trade was favored by its privileged geographical position at the heart of a region midway between Babylonia and the Western countries and between the Mediterranean and the Persian Gulf.

Between 2000 and 1750 B.C., Mari reached the height of its glory, acting as a true regional capital, before it was destroyed by the armies of Hammurabi.

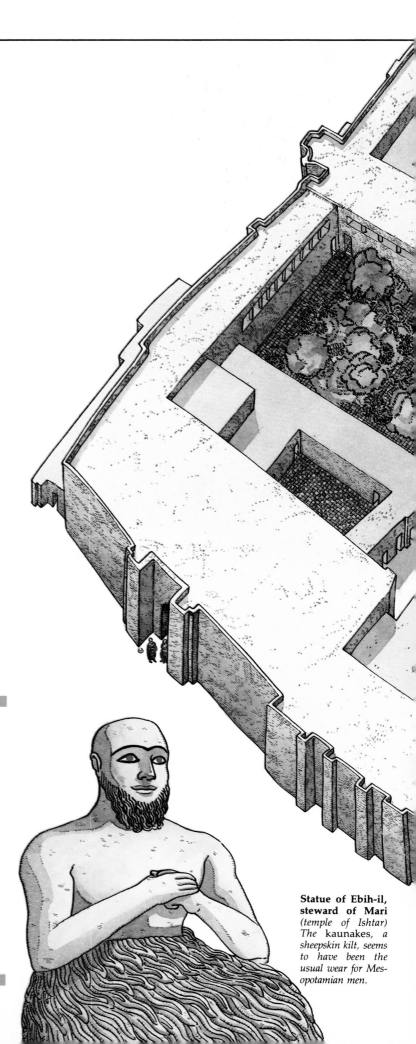

Statue of Ebih-il, steward of Mari (temple of Ishtar) The kaunakes, a sheepskin kilt, seems to have been the usual wear for Mesopotamian men.

ANIMAL SACRIFICE

Fragment of one of the wall paintings found in the palace of Mari, now in the Louvre Museum in Paris. The brilliant colors, which were painted on a thick coat of white plaster, cover the full range of yellows, browns, and oranges. A bull, decorated for the ceremony, is being taken to the sacrifice. The tips of its horns are coated in silver and it has a ring through its nose.

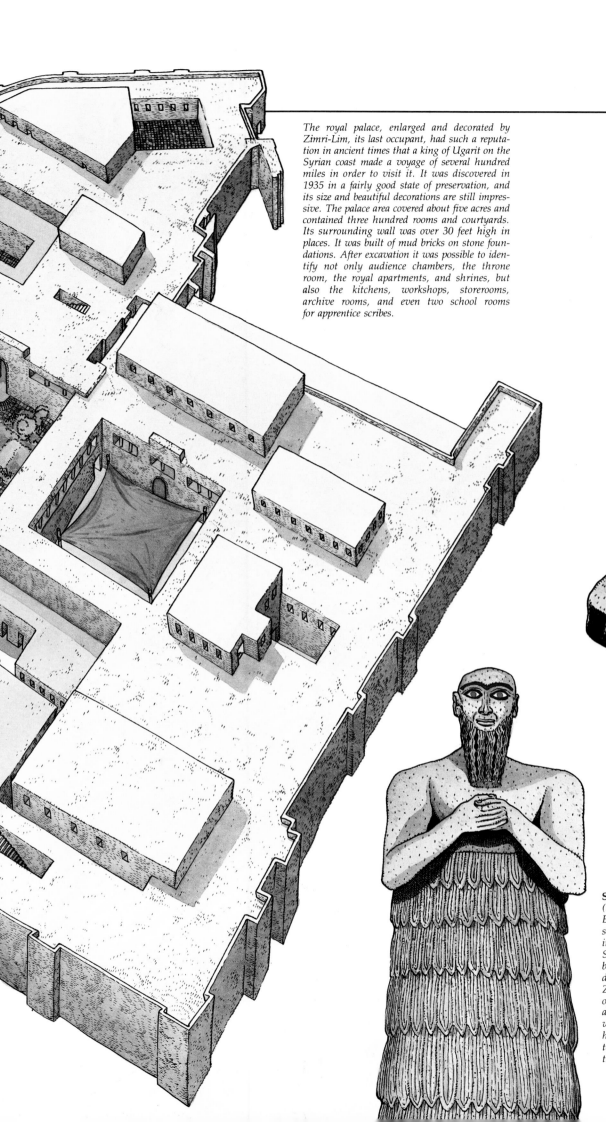

The royal palace, enlarged and decorated by Zimri-Lim, its last occupant, had such a reputation in ancient times that a king of Ugarit on the Syrian coast made a voyage of several hundred miles in order to visit it. It was discovered in 1935 in a fairly good state of preservation, and its size and beautiful decorations are still impressive. The palace area covered about five acres and contained three hundred rooms and courtyards. Its surrounding wall was over 30 feet high in places. It was built of mud bricks on stone foundations. After excavation it was possible to identify not only audience chambers, the throne room, the royal apartments, and shrines, but also the kitchens, workshops, storerooms, archive rooms, and even two school rooms for apprentice scribes.

Goddess with a flowing vase
This splendid statue, nearly life-size, was found in two pieces in the palace of Zimri-Lim. The eyes have lost their shell and lapis lazuli inlays, and the nose has been broken. We know she is a goddess by the horns on her headdress.

A remarkable feature of this statue is that it has a channel drilled through it from the base to the vase so that water can flow from it—providing a living demonstration of the goddess's gift of life giving water.

Statue of Shibum
(temple of Ninni-Zaza)
Engraved on the back of this statue can be read the following inscription: "For the life of Ikun-Shamagan, king of Mari, Shibum, chief surveyor, has dedicated his statue to Ninni-Zaza." Shibum was an important official, second in rank in the palace. By having himself sculpted with his hands joined in prayer, he was demonstrating his loyalty to the king and his devotion to the god.

LIFE IN THE SWAMPS

espite the farmers' continual hard work, the great plain of Mesopotamia was far from completely cultivated. There was too much water for it all to be controlled. Carefully tended farmlands lay side by side with great swamps, where wildlife lived in abundance.

There, since the earliest times (from the fifth millennium B.C.), men and women had lived—and still do—at the heart of a maze of tall reeds that could only be circumnavigated by boat. The reeds, 13 to 16 feet high, not only camouflaged the huts and villages, but were also used to build them. The foundations were made by building up alternate layers of woven reeds and mud on the spongy surface of the marshland. Floors, roofs, and walls were then made using woven reeds, and bunches of reeds were tied into tight bundles sturdy enough to serve as supporting posts and beams.

The marshlands of southern Iraq, as seen today. People still live there in reed huts that have been built in the same way for thousands of years.

The swamps were inhabited by a large number of wild creatures. Among them big buffalo lived half submerged, luxuriating in the still, muddy waters. But above all there were all kinds of birds—ducks, pelicans, herons, kingfishers, and flamingos.

The townspeople particularly enjoyed eating some of them, so the birds provided a considerable source of income for the people who lived in the marsh.

Boats were made of long reeds woven together. The people's main occupations were fishing and hunting. The swamp waters, like the rivers and canals, were full of fish, and the Mesopotamians were skilled at catching them. The fishermen would go out alone in canoes or in groups aboard a round fishing boat, which they propelled by pushing a pole against the muddy bottom (the marsh waters were scarcely more than 20 inches deep). They would spend hours on the calm waters with their lines, nets, and baskets. When evening came, the boats would gather together, and a small portion of the catch would be distributed among the local people. The rest was taken by canal to the river, where it was bought by traders who took it, usually by raft, to be sold in village markets.

TOWN LIFE

It is not easy to give an accurate description of the big Mesopotamian towns and what went on in them. Little remains of their mud-brick houses, and one needs a good deal of learning, as well as a vivid imagination, to picture what daily life there was like. Some of the towns were huge. A primitive town like Uruk may have reached a population of 50,000—which was not small in size—and capital cities like Ur must have been much bigger.

The built-up area of Ur covered 1,400 acres, with an average of about 110 houses to 100 acres. There were probably six people to a house, including children and servants. So archaeologists estimate that the total population was a minimum of 250,000 and a maximum of 400,000 at the end of the third millennium B.C.!

Let us try to imagine a town like this. Its streets are full of people, jostling, meeting, and greeting each other. Most of the men have full, curly beards and bare chests. They wear loincloths tied at the waist and rolled up around the thighs or reaching to the knees or even the ankles, depending on current fashion, the season, and individual taste. The women, very conscious of their appearance, dress in light, brightly colored robes fastened at the shoulder and leaving the right arm free.

Both men and women adore jewelry, and everyone owns a collection of rings, collars, earrings, lucky charms, and bracelets, the materials depending on the wealth of the wearer. There are even some excellent imitations of gold and turquoise.

People pass each other in the narrow, twisting streets, some of them small alleyways leading to groups of houses. There is no sewerage system; garbage is burned at the back of the houses or simply thrown out to litter the streets.

From the outside the houses of Ur must have presented a varied sight. Two- and three-story dwellings stood alongside single-story houses; none of them were built in a straight line. In general the facades were made of fired bricks as far as the ground-floor ceiling, and sun-dried bricks were used above that. The houses had few openings—a low door onto the street and a few air vents that scarcely qualified as windows. For the people of Ur, protection from the burning heat and dust clouds must have been of prime importance. These generally roomy and well furnished houses were owned not by aristocrats but by middle-class people like merchants, shop-keepers, and traders.

Even so, Ur had its poorer quarters. Some much smaller houses have also been found; since they were close to the large shrines, they may well have housed the temple slaves.

Most of the houses were built around an inner courtyard onto which faced the kitchen and living room as well as the servants' and guests' rooms. A wooden staircase led to the upper floor and to a covered wooden gallery supported by four corner posts. This gallery led to other rooms, probably the bedrooms of the people living in the house. The gallery was overhung by a slightly sloping roof, but above the courtyard a large opening let in light and air. To help keep the house cool and to make it brighter, the interior and sometimes the exterior walls were coated with white plaster.

ENDLESS WARFARE

The strong defensive walls around Uruk, Kish, Lagash, Ur, and Mari show just how preoccupied the Mesopotamian peoples were with warfare. Imagine the massive amount of work that must have gone into surrounding Uruk with a 6-mile wall 5,000 years ago.

The tablets and inscriptions discovered during excavations attest to the frequency of conflicts in Sumeria, both civil wars to determine local supremacy and defensive struggles against foreign invaders.

The most warlike of these invaders were the Guti, a barbarian tribe who invaded from the mountains to the east; in 2230 B.C. they began subjecting Mesopotamia to the fire and the sword, cutting off roads and canals, ravaging the countryside, and burning down towns. The motivation for such attacks was mainly economic; the leaders wanted to gain control of the great commercial routes and the most fertile farmlands.

But there was another consideration, too. We know that the title *King of Kish* was prized above all others, since it designated that its holder was the rightful ruler of all Mesopotamia. To be king there was a prize worthy of any risk, and ambitious warrior-kings assiduously played power politics to reach the top. The recently discovered archives of the town of Ebla, in northern Syria, refer to the complicated play of alliances and the violence of the warfare. Allusions to sacking and pillage and to the mountains of dead bodies the conquerors left in their trail show how bitter the conflicts were.

Other documents describe how the armies were organized. They were solidly staffed by officers under the supreme command of the king, whose duty it was to take part in battle. Most of the soldiers were probably professionals, but plans existed for mobilizing civilians and, if necessary, citizens were brought in to swell the ranks of the regular army.

Sometimes, prisoners of war were also forced to join the victorious army and go into battle. But they could also meet other fates. Large groups of them might be put to death to demoralize the enemy, in which case their heads were piled in pyramids at the gates of cities. Or they could be kept as slaves and employed as forced labor, digging canals or building temples. They might even be used as a means of exchange when peace returned. Buying back prisoners was a common practice, which enabled armies to put themselves back on their feet—and start hostilities all over again.

The warlike deeds and triumphs of conquerors were celebrated in works of art. The most famous is the splendid "Stele of the Vultures" in the Louvre Museum, which dates from 2500 B.C. Unfortunately, only a fragment of it has survived. It shows the soldiers of Lagash advancing into battle in a phalanx, led by their king, sword in hand. His warriors are trampling the corpses of the enemy while vultures prepare to tear their flesh. The lower register shows the light infantry marching bare-chested, spears over their shoulders. The king is still at their head, but this time he is in his war chariot, brandishing a javelin. Between these two scenes of war, cuneiform inscriptions celebrate the glory of the victorious army.

Around 3000 B.C. the Sumerians started to use a technological innovation that promised to have a splendid future: the wheel. Its first use was, it seems, as a part of the process of making pottery. Thanks to the wheel, the lathe that allows the potter to make beautiful and exactly shaped vases was developed. Quite soon thereafter the technology was applied to the needs of transportation. The most ancient wagon wheels discovered were solid disks made from three pieces of wood. Some wagons with such wheels were excavated at Ur. In the beginning, bulls and onagers (large wild asses) were hitched to the wagons. It was a millennium later (about 2000 B.C.) that horses were used. In the meantime, soldiers became interested in these vehicles. Since they were at first crudely made, heavy, and easily broken, the chariots of war were used mainly to impress the enemy and to pursue those fleeing battle. With the invention of the spoked wheel the chariots were much lighter and much sturdier; they then became a completely separate tactical weapon that was necessary to the conduct of warfare.

HOW WRITING BEGAN AT SUMER

Like the control of fire and the development of agriculture, the invention of writing was one of the most decisive events of human history. An outstanding means of communication, writing has enabled language and thought to be permanently recorded; it acts as humanity's memory.

Writing was invented nearly 5,000 years ago in Mesopotamia, at a time when the Sumerian civilization had reached a very high level. The Sumerian economy was based on cereal growing and cattle rearing, and there was a need for a strict control of the goods being put into circulation. It was the task of the priests to keep a centralized store of farm produce, which had to be redistributed to the various temples; they began to keep accounts of all these riches. For every product the priests registered—wheat, barley, goats, oxen, and so on—they made a mark on a tablet of wet clay, followed by a stylized picture of the item. In this way they evolved a script based on pictograms (from the Latin *pictus,* "a drawing," and the Greek *gramma,* "a letter").

Pictographic writing enabled the priests to translate into signs a large number of words in current usage—those, at least, that were connected with concrete objects that could be drawn. However, it did not permit them to express ideas or describe complex situations, or to write grammatical sentences. So it occurred to the Sumerians to replace drawings of things by signs that would represent sounds.

These *phonograms* were the ancestors of our letters, which also relate to sounds. Since phonograms could convey ideas, they made it possible to write sentences in which the words appeared in their correct relationship. And since the same sound might occur in several different words, the number of signs could be considerably reduced—from one thousand to three hundred. Around 3000 B.C. the transition from a pictorial to a symbolic form of writing, known as cuneiform (wedge-shaped), had been completed.

A diorite weight signed by Shu-Sin, fourth king of the third dynasty of Ur (2037 B.C.–2029 B.C.). As always with hard stone, the engraving is simple and legible. The inscription, in Sumerian, states: "Five mines, certified. Shu-Sin, strong king, king of Ur, king of four regions."

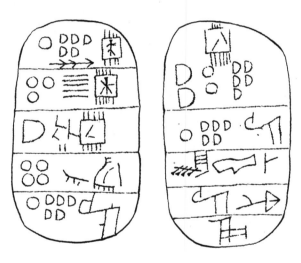

A clay tablet from Lagash enumerating goats and sheep. The numbers, written in ancient Sumerian, are easy to translate: the small conical signs correspond to the number 1, the large ones to 60, and the circles to 10.

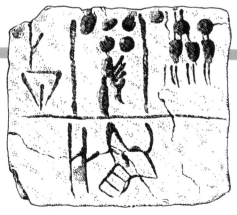

CLAY TABLETS

For the privileged, Mesopotamian writing was inscribed on clay. Fired or simply dried in the sun, it was an excellent way of preserving documents. It was used for the most important political and religious texts and also for administrative documents and private correspondence. This pictographic tablet found at Kish is one of the oldest we have, dating from the end of the fourth millennium B.C. The tablet was probably an accounting document. Three of the drawings are easy to make out—a woman, an animal, and some wheat.

In the precincts of the temple of Uruk, scribes register the arrival of a flock of sheep.

When a temple or palace was built, large nails of clay were set into the walls. Only the nail tops were visible; they commemorated the founding of the new building. The first (2400 B.C.) records a fraternal treaty between Lagash and Uruk. The second (2150 B.C.) honors the new temple dedicated to Ningirsu, the guardian god of Lagash.

DECIPHERING CUNEIFORM

After their days of glory, the Sumerian and Babylonian empires suffered a long decline and were eventually destroyed. The memory of their existence nearly faded away altogether. Nothing, or nearly nothing, was left of their formidable pasts. Little by little the ruins of the cities, burned and razed over and over again, were buried in sand. Only a few bricks covered with inscriptions and sketches of the ruined walls made by travelers drew the attention of scholars to a long-forgotten form of writing. Thomas Hyde, Professor of Hebrew at Oxford University, was struck by the angular look of the script, and in 1700 he gave it the name *cuneiform*, from the Latin *cuneus*, meaning "wedge." It was not until the next century, however, that its secret was revealed through an amazing piece of work carried out by another Englishman, Henry Creswicke Rawlinson.

Rawlinson was a diplomat who in 1826 was sent to India, where he learned Hindi, Arabic, and modern Persian. He was then sent to Persia, where in 1833 he decided to tackle the task of deciphering cuneiform writing. However, he was called back to England and had to wait thirteen years before returning to the Near East to pursue his enterprise. In 1846 he was at last able to examine the cliff at Bīsitūn in southwest Iran; on its face, 400 feet above the ground, a gigantic display of sculpture and inscriptions celebrated the victories of Darius I, king of the Persians, in the fifth century B.C. Rawlinson realized that the thousands of signs were versions of the same text written in three different languages, including ancient Persian! Fired with enthusiasm, he began patiently to copy the lengthy trilingual inscription. He worked under perilous conditions, perched at the top of a ladder, clinging to the rock face with his left hand while holding a notebook and pencil in his right!

As he had foreseen, Rawlinson managed to decipher the Persian text without too much difficulty, followed by the second text, in Elamite. But fifty years were to go by before the third language was unraveled. It was Akkadian, the direct descendant of ancient Sumerian, the oldest form of writing known in the history of humans.

The law code of Hammurabi, king of Babylon, drawn up about 1760 B.C., is famous in the history of writing. Several copies of it were inscribed on basalt stelae (stone slabs) 6 feet high and weighing 4 tons. The copies were erected in large towns to remind people to respect the law. At the top the king is shown worshiping a god, probably Shamash, god of the sun and of justice. Below are thirty-five hundred lines set out in vertical columns, celebrating the great king's accession to power and his decisions concerning the law. Various sections deal with theft, agricultural work, trade, the family, marriage, inheritance, children, and slaves. It concludes with the epilogue: "These are the just decisions that Hammurabi, wise king, has made in order to establish firm discipline and good conduct in his land."

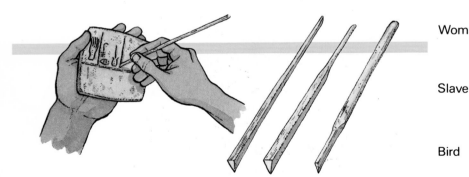

THE SCRIBE'S WRITING IMPLEMENTS

To write on soft clay, the scribes used small styluses cut from reeds. They were shaped at the end according to the script to be used: a triangular tip for cuneiform, a narrow tip for dots and dashes, and a round one for writing the numbers of the archaic period.

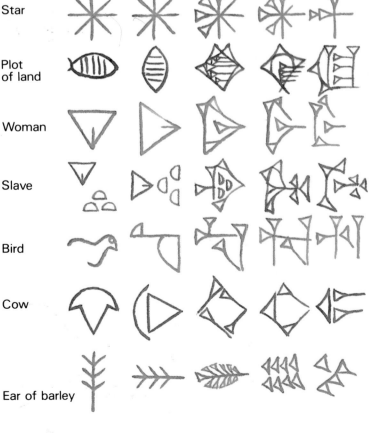

The development of Mesopotamian writing from pictogram to cuneiform. Around 2800 B.C. the scribes began writing in horizontal lines instead of columns. As a result, the signs were moved a quarter turn to the right quickly.

Star

Plot of land

Woman

Slave

Bird

Cow

Ear of barley

Numbers

D	𒁹	1
DD	𒐀	2
DDD	𒐁	3
DD DD	𒐂	4
DDD DD	𒐅	5
O	𒌋	10
D	𒐕	60
⊙D	𒐏	600
O	◇	3,600
◎	◇	36,000

To write, you need something to write on. In Mesopotamia, where stone and wood were rare, clay was the most convenient material. The scribe used tablets of wet clay. With swift, easy movements he made impressions with a stylus, which varied in shape and could be held at different angles. Once inscribed, the tablets were dried in the sun or baked in a kiln. They were then practically indestructible.

EGYPTIAN HIEROGLYPHS

Writing appeared in Egypt almost at the same time as in Sumeria, around 3200 B.C., probably in response to similar economic, political, and religious needs. Ever since, people have been fascinated by its beauty. Writing enriches the temple walls, statues, obelisks, and funerary objects on which it is found, with a poetry whose meaning was a mystery for many centuries. The ancient Greeks, impressed by the originality and complexity of this writing system, gave it the name *hieroglyphes*, "sacred pictures." When they were finally deciphered in 1822 by a French Egyptologist, Jean François Champollion, they lost none of their mysterious charm. A form of communication was revealed which was as practical as it was artistic and as precise as it was elegant.

Hieroglyphs were generally used for solemn inscriptions, usually carved on monuments and intended to last. But the ancient Egyptians also used lesser known forms of writing: cursive (flowing) scripts, quicker and easier to write, were used as much as if not more than hieroglyphic script in daily life.

Hieratic writing was used by scribes, usually on papyrus, for administrative and legal documents, for treatises on medicine and magic, and also for private correspondence.

Demotic, or popular, writing, set out horizontally from right to left, was even more flowing. It did not appear until the ninth century B.C. and was a simplified form of hieratic writing, which it completely replaced some centuries later. It is reported that the last "House of Life" in which the scribes passed on the knowledge of hieroglyphic writing was closed in the fourth century B.C. But hieroglyphic writing survived, for it was found on the Rosetta stone of the second century B.C. and on Egyptian temples built in the period of the Roman Empire, that is, for at least 2 or 3 centuries into our era. The demotic writing probably was replaced over the centuries with the adoption of alphabetic writing, the Coptic script, and the knowledge of hieroglyphs disappeared with the triumph of Christianity in the fifth century A.D.

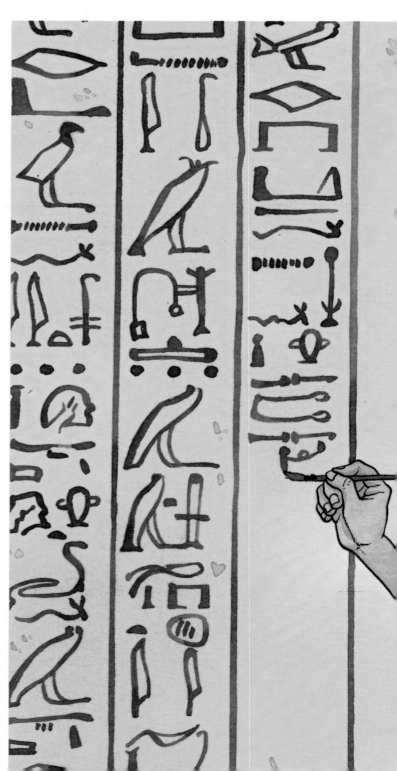

Hieratic script

Hieroglyphic transcription

Demotic script

Hieroglyphic transcription

"SPEECH OF THE GODS"

The Egyptians called their hieroglyphs "the speech of the gods." They attributed their creation to the ibis-headed moon god, Thoth. Thoth, who was already represented as a monkey, was god of writing and numbers, and the patron of scribes. The scribes worshiped him with great devotion, as shown in this statue of Nebmertuf, priest-archivist and royal scribe to Pharaoh Amenhotep III (around 1400 B.C.).

The pharaoh took a great deal of trouble to prepare his last resting place, employing the finest architects, sculptors, painters, and cabinetmakers. Here artists are at work decorating the walls of the royal tomb. The master painter has sketched a design and is copying it onto the wall. His assistants are preparing the colors to be applied to it.

In ancient Egypt a copy of The Book of the Dead would be placed in the dead person's tomb. This was a roll of papyrus decorated with beautiful pictures. The priest would read the text at the funeral, and the book was then left with the dead person for eternity. Most of it described the stages which the soul had to go through to be reborn. Like the sun, which daily dies and reappears, the soul had to pass through shadows to return to the light. The most fearful stage was appearing before Osiris, god of the dead. He listened to the person's confession and weighed his heart. If the god acquitted the person, he or she was sent in peace to enjoy the delights of a heavenly afterlife.

The principles of Egyptian writing

Like Sumerian writing in its early stages, Egyptian writing was based on pictograms, each sign representing a specific thing. But unlike Sumerian writing, which rapidly became more abstract, hieroglyphs changed amazingly little until the end of the time of the pharoahs. Classical Egyptian, which was used at the beginning of the second millennium B.C., comprises seven hundred signs depicting an enormous variety of creatures and objects—people, animals, plants, tools, buildings, and so on. These are ideograms, signs conveying ideas. To a certain extent they could convey actions. To write the verb to run, the scribes would draw a man running; for to see, they drew an eye. But how were they to express abstract ideas and feelings, such as remember, love, and regret?

Like the Sumerians, the Egyptians adopted phonograms, or sound signs, but at the same time they retained the principle of word-pictures, using the rebus, that is, a sound conveyed by drawing an object whose name sounds exactly the same. Thus, in English the word belief would be written by drawing first a bee and then a leaf.

The scribes also made use of a third group of signs, called determinatives. When a word could have two possible meanings, a sign was added to it to distinguish which one was intended. Thus, words conveying the notion of strength were followed by an arm in armor; words conveying abstract ideas were followed by a sealed roll of papyrus. There are around a hundred of these signs. Although it may seem complex, Egyptian writing is relatively easy to read once you know what all the symbols mean. In fact, it is much easier to read than many other ancient scripts.

49

THE FIRST ALPHABETS

The word *alphabet* comes from the Greek. It is made up of the first two Greek letters, *alpha* and *beta*. The use of this word indicates the extent of Greek influence in the development of modern languages. But it would be a mistake to regard the Greeks as the inventors of the alphabet. Many centuries before the appearance of the Greek alphabet, two genuine alphabets had already seen the light of day at the eastern end of the Mediterranean, on the coast of Phoenicia.

In antiquity the Phoenicians had settled at a meeting point, for both land and sea routes, between several civilizations—Mesopotamia, Egypt, the land of the Hittites, Cyprus, and Crete. Starting as skilled farmers, they became leading traders and seafarers. They could be seen on all the caravan routes and even more at all the eastern Mediterranean ports.

For several centuries Phoenician scribes wrote to their clients, using the forms of writing most current, cuneiform and hieroglyphs, for their orders and accounts. But these very busy traders found these scripts, involving a large number of symbols, laborious to write. At the end of the second millennium B.C. it was decided to create a simplified system that would cut down on the number of penstrokes needed. Their first efforts were not a success, but the idea of a simpler system developed. Around 1500 B.C. the cuneiform alphabet of Ugarit was produced, a great achievement. It consisted, to start, of thirty letters, all based on Mesopotamian writing; they were later reduced to twenty-two.

The alphabet itself, the system of writing sounds, must not be confused with the different languages that made use of it. At Ugarit (now in Syria), archaeologists have found thousands of tablets written in several languages—Ugaritic itself (close to Hebrew), Aramaic, Phoenician, and also Akkadian—all using this one alphabet!

The alphabet was an innovation that vastly increased the spread of knowledge, for it made knowledge accessible to a greater number of people. Only an educated elite could learn seven hundred signs, but almost anyone could remember twenty or thirty and learn to put them together.

Five axeheads like this provided the key to the first alphabet, the alphabet of Ungarit. In 1929 a German, Bauer, and a Frenchman, Virolleaud, ascertained that the text on the blade designated the name of the object and its owner. When the thirty-letter alphabet had been reconstructed, thousands of texts could be translated.

A	a	alpha	I	j	iota	P	r	rô
B	b	bêta	K	k	kappa	Σ	s	sigma
Γ	g	gamma	Λ	l	lambda	T	t	tau
Δ	d	delta	M	m	mu	Y	u	upsilon
E	e	êpsilon	N	n	nu	Φ	ph	phi
Z	z	dzêta	Ξ	x	xi	X	kh	khi
H	ē	êta	O	o	omikron	Ψ	ps	psi
Θ	th	thêta	Π	p	pi	Ω	ō	omêga

When the Greeks launched themselves "on the back of the vast ocean" (Homer), they came into contact with their Cretan, Cypriot, and Phoenician neighbors. They adopted the Phoenician alphabet, but unlike Phoenician vowels, Greek vowels needed to be written down. So the Greeks cleverly took the Phoenician consonants they did not need and turned them into vowels.

Toward the end of the twelfth century B.C., a twenty-two–character alphabet began to be used. The oldest example of this linear writing was found on the lid of the sarcophagus of Ahiram, king of Byblos in the eleventh century B.C. This development very likely resulted from a change of writing material. Clay tablets were replaced by papyrus or ostraca (pieces of pottery). Brushes and pens became the most suitable writing implements for these smooth surfaces, and writing techniques changed, becoming finer and more flowing. The Phoenician alphabet became incredibly popular almost as soon as it appeared. The Phoenicians were great travelers, and they "exported" their writing with their other merchandise. Several nations adopted it for writing their languages—Aramaic, ancient Hebrew, Moabite, and Punic. Other races, like the Greeks, used the writing as a basis for alphabets of their own. Byblos itself faded away, but its writing was the basis for nearly all the alphabets of the world. And its name lives on in words like Bible, bibliography and bibliophile.

CHINESE WRITING

Chinese writing came fifteen centuries after the scripts of Mesopotamia and Egypt. The oldest specimens, discovered near the banks of the Yellow River, go back to about 1500 B.C. and consist of religious texts inscribed on animal bones or tortoiseshells. But unlike Sumerian and Egyptian writing, which disappeared long ago, Chinese writing is still in use.

Its long life is explained by the structure of the Chinese language. Chinese speech is monosyllabic, that is to say every word consists of a single syllable. In a society as highly evolved as the Chinese, the spoken language requires thousands of words, whereas the human voice can only produce around a hundred syllables! So, to avoid confusion, the Chinese use tones, or different modulations, as well as gestures and mimicry. To enable this language to be written, the only solution was to create a different sign for every single word to make sure that it was correctly identified.

Most of the basic symbols were easily recognizable drawings. The sun was represented by a circle with a line in it, the moon by a crescent. Man was pictured standing on the ground (*li*), in profile (*jen*), or imprisoned (*ts'iu*). As the centuries went by, these signs changed, though some remained fairly close to the original pictogram. As in Sumer, as the Chinese language became more complex, pictographic writing had to be abandoned and a phonetic value given to the symbols. In the Chinese language today, the vast majority of symbols—which are called characters—are formed by a mixture of meaning and sound. As the phonetics of the language have also changed considerably over the centuries, it is impossible for a reader to guess the exact pronunciation of a word he or she doesn't know! What is more, different dialects use different pronunciations. Someone from Peking in the north and a Cantonese from the south will not be able to understand each other. However, they can communicate through writing, since this is exactly the same for both dialects, so people from different regions can understand the meaning of a written word, even if they don't know how to say it. Chinese characters play a role similar to that of our Arabic and Roman numerals: The signs 4 or IV can be perfectly understood by an American, a Frenchman, or a German, even though they are pronounced, respectively, "four," "quatre," and "vier."

The defect of this remarkable system is that learning to write in China is very hard work. The schoolchild doesn't have just twenty-six letters to learn, but several thousand characters. The number of known characters was around two thousand at the time of Confucius (in the fifth century B.C.); by the end of the Han dynasty (second century A.D.) it was over fifteen thousand, and in the seventeenth century it was nearly forty thousand! Today you need to know thirty-five hundred words to read a newspaper, five thousand to six thousand to reach college standards, and around ten thousand to understand classical literature!

The art of calligraphy was the prerogative of the privileged in China. It was not a profession but a discipline practiced by the educated, intellectual elite. To write beautiful characters was to be in harmony with the world, and Chinese poets and writers most often sought their inspiration in nature.

The first written Chinese texts were engraved on bones or tortoise shells (1500 B.C.). During the Ch'in Dynasty and the early Han Dynasty (third and second centuries B.C.), people mainly wrote on wood and bamboo. Silk, which was very expensive, was reserved for important documents. According to tradition, it was in 105 A.D. that paper was invented by a eunuch of the imperial palace. It was made by reducing plant fibers to a paste, which was stretched and dried to form a thin sheet. The Chinese used a variety of materials in papermaking—fibrous plants like hemp, jute, flax, and mulberry bark, and grass-type plants like bamboo, reeds, rice stalks, and even cotton.

CALLIGRAPHY

A character is made up of a specific number of strokes, between one and thirty. All the characters, however complex, must occupy an equal amount of space within an imaginary square. They must be written according to a strict order. Traditionally, they are laid out in vertical columns and read from top to bottom, beginning on the right-hand page. Above are seven lines which make up a Chinese character, with arrows showing the direction they are drawn in. These lines can be found, for example, in the character fa, meaning "The law." The numbers indicate the order the characters must be written in.

	Sun	Moon	Rain	Horse	Man	Prisoner	Mountain	Wood
Around 1500 B.C.								
Around 200 B.C.								
Today								

How some Chinese characters have evolved from the original pictograms

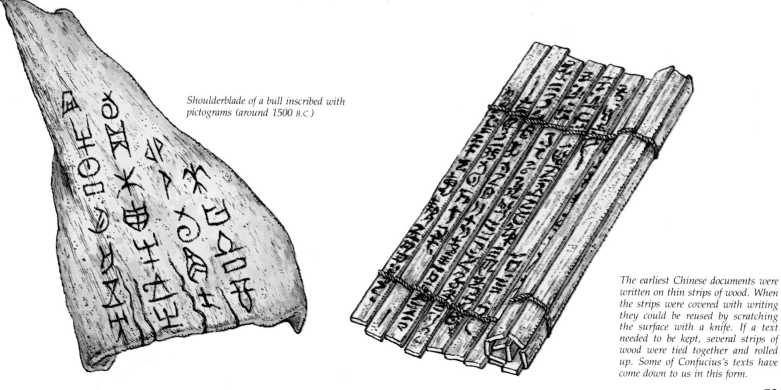

Shoulderblade of a bull inscribed with pictograms (around 1500 B.C.)

The earliest Chinese documents were written on thin strips of wood. When the strips were covered with writing they could be reused by scratching the surface with a knife. If a text needed to be kept, several strips of wood were tied together and rolled up. Some of Confucius's texts have come down to us in this form.

53

THE INDUS VALLEY

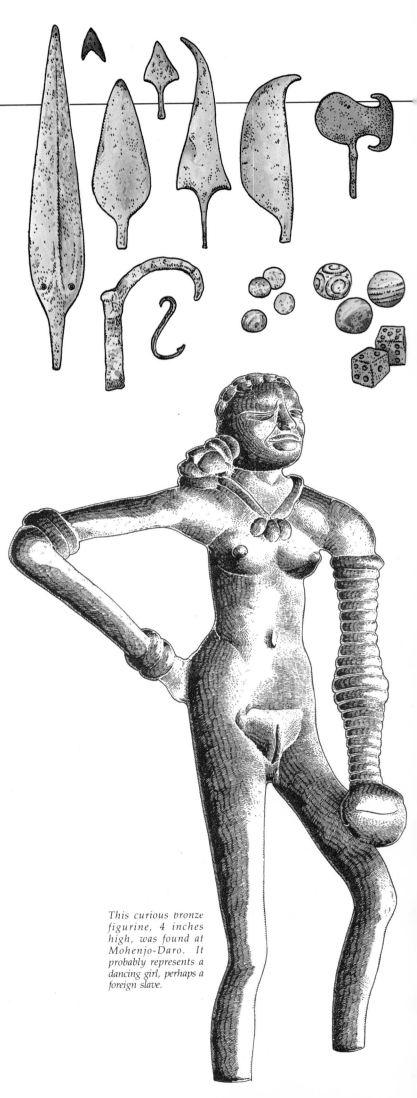

Between 2500 B.C. and 1700 B.C., at the time when Mesopotamia and Egypt were reaching the height of their glory, a third great center of culture was developing in the Indus Basin in northwestern India.

The Indus Valley civilization had totally vanished from human memory when it came to light again in the 1920s with the excavation of two great cities, Harappa in the Punjab and Mohenjo-Daro in the Sind. All that remained of Harappa was a jumble of ruins. But so much information was gathered from Mohenjo-Daro that it was possible to reconstruct the history of this fabulous empire of unsuspected magnitude.

At the beginning of the third millennium, some people came from what is now Iran and settled in the Indus Valley, bringing with them a technology new to the region. They were remarkably skilled in both agriculture and metallurgy; they used writing and an advanced system of weights and measures. It is believed that they had developed these skills as a result of earlier contacts with the Sumerians. Within a few centuries the Indus Valley had a large, mainly agricultural population. The peasant farmers bred a wide variety of animals, including buffalo, zebus, sheep, and pigs, and used oxen, horses, and donkeys as beasts of burden. They grew wheat, barley, peas, rice, and melons; they made sesame oil, and in the south they grew cotton.

Although the climate was dry, the crops grew in abundance. The thick layer of silt left by the waters of the Indus enriched the soil, and in the dry season there were numerous canals to irrigate the fields. After the harvest the produce was taken to the towns and stored in communal depots, huge granaries built inside the great fortified citadels. The city's treasuries of wheat and rice had to be protected at all costs from floods and thieves. In winter the town authorities handed out regular allotments of grain. There was no money; laborers, craftworkers, and town officials were all paid in grain.

There were smiths skilled in copper, bronze, and lead working. Others worked with gold, silver, and semiprecious stones like agate and carnelian. They made jewels, ornaments, toys, and small stone seals finely incised with animal motifs.

From big ports like Lotha, some 370 miles from Mohenjo-Daro, seafarers and merchants established profitable trading links with both nearby countries and more distant lands like Mesopotamia. In several Sumerian ports, clay tablets have been found, registering the arrival of ships laden with gold, silver, copper, tin, wood, and ivory brought from the land of Meloukkha. It seems more than likely that this word, which means nothing today, was the name then given to the Indus Valley.

This curious bronze figurine, 4 inches high, was found at Mohenjo-Daro. It probably represents a dancing girl, perhaps a foreign slave.

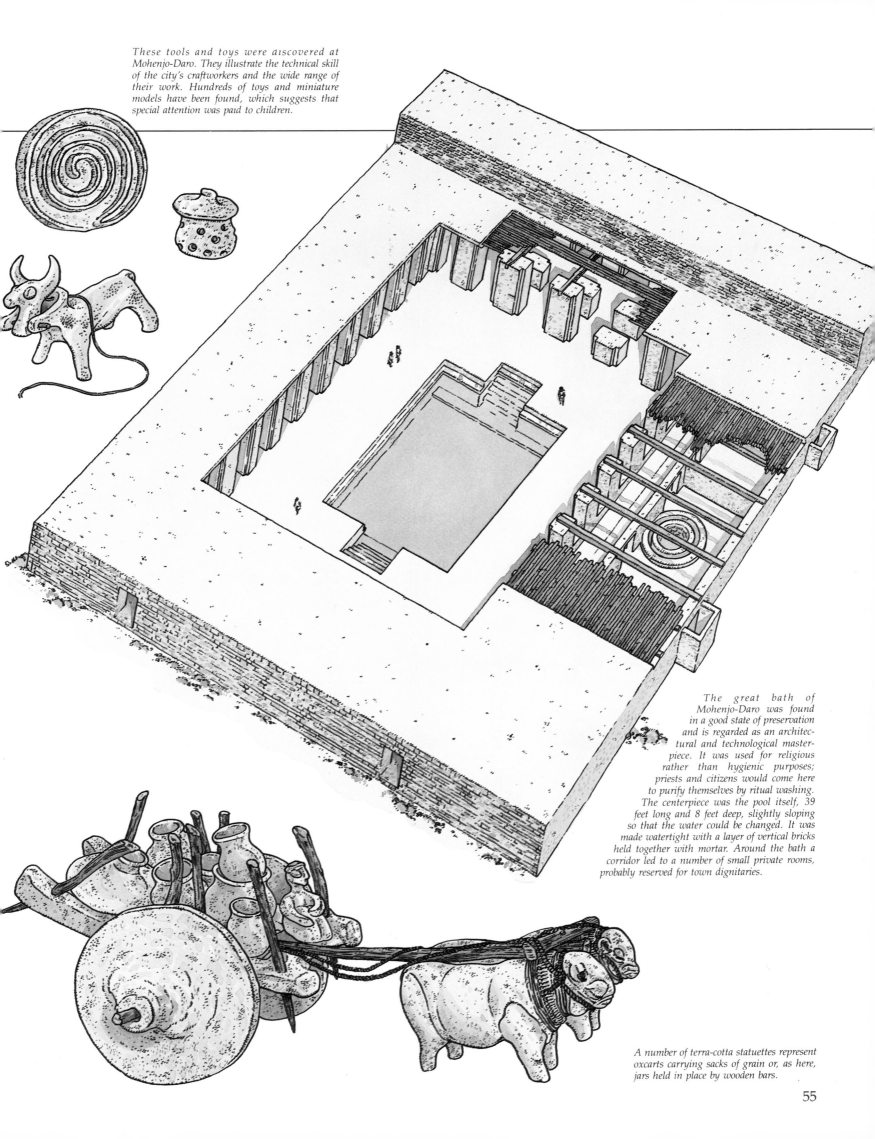

These tools and toys were discovered at Mohenjo-Daro. They illustrate the technical skill of the city's craftworkers and the wide range of their work. Hundreds of toys and miniature models have been found, which suggests that special attention was paid to children.

The great bath of Mohenjo-Daro was found in a good state of preservation and is regarded as an architectural and technological masterpiece. It was used for religious rather than hygienic purposes; priests and citizens would come here to purify themselves by ritual washing. The centerpiece was the pool itself, 39 feet long and 8 feet deep, slightly sloping so that the water could be changed. It was made watertight with a layer of vertical bricks held together with mortar. Around the bath a corridor led to a number of small private rooms, probably reserved for town dignitaries.

A number of terra-cotta statuettes represent oxcarts carrying sacks of grain or, as here, jars held in place by wooden bars.

MOHENJO-DARO

Harappa and Mohenjo-Daro were the largest cities in the Indus Valley. Although some 350 miles apart, they are very similar in size, layout, and building styles. In their heyday, each had a population of at least 40,000. All the indications are that they were capitals, but we do not know if one had authority over the other, or whether they were exactly contemporary. The Indus Empire may well have been big enough to require the existence of twin capitals.

Mohenjo-Daro lay on the north bank of the Indus. In the lower part of the town, houses, shops, and craftworkers' workshops lay along great avenues laid out from north to south and cut at right angles by minor streets and lanes. Between these thoroughfares were square blocks of nearly identical houses served by an excellent drainage system. The upper town, the citadel, was built high on a massive mud and mud-brick platform and surrounded by thick walls; it contained huge communal buildings—a great bath, a granary, and an assembly hall for political meetings.

Among the great buildings of Mohenjo-Daro, there is no palace and no temple, and we know nothing about the city's administration or religious practices. Unlike the Sumerians, Egyptians, and Chinese, the people of the Indus civilization seem to have been unconcerned about life after death. The few tombs that have been found contain nothing that would be of use to the dead in an afterlife.

Some skeletons were found in the streets, clearly left to lie unburied where they fell: this raises the question of how Mohenjo-Daro came to an end. Some historians believe the town was ransacked in 1500 B.C. by invading Arians, a barbarian tribe from the mountains of Afghanistan, after which it was deserted. Other scholars favor the theory of a natural disaster, such as a gradual but inexorable flood that forced the last inhabitants to abandon the town after several years of vain struggle to control the rising waters.

The writing of the Indus people remains a mystery. Although several attempts have been made, no one has succeeded in interpreting the pictograms that appear on seals like this one. At Mohenjo-Daro, clay and steatite stamps were used to seal goods and identify thier owners; stamps were also carried as lucky charms. Many of them were decorated with animal designs.

A number of female statues have been found at Mohenjo-Daro. These statues give the impression that the citizens set great store by hairdressing. Only a part of this statue has been preserved. Traces of soot in the hollow part indicate that it was used as a lamp.

A CLEAN CITY

Some archaeologists have nicknamed Mohenjo-Daro the "Manhattan of the Bronze Age." Like many modern cities, the capital of the Indus Valley was laid out on a strict grid plan, allowing no room for deviations. Blocks of rectangular buildings were divided into islands by main arterial roads several hundred yards long and at least 30 feet wide. The citizens must have been very conscious of hygiene, for there was an elaborate drainage system, and at some crossroads there were places for dumping garbage.

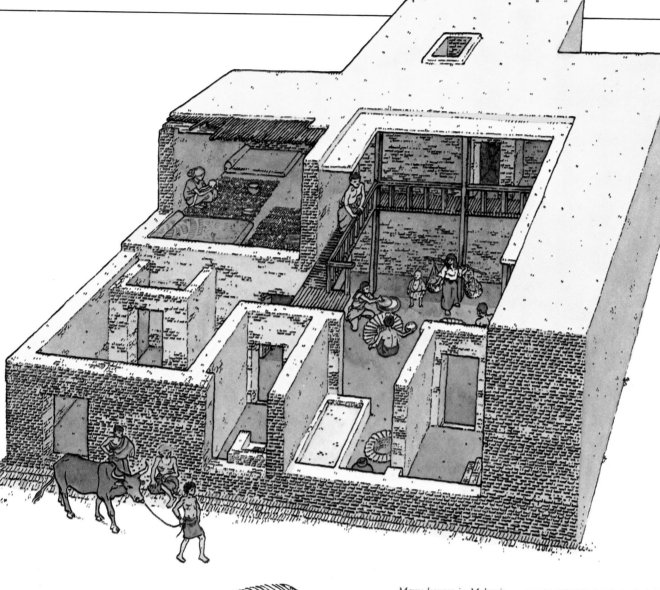

Most of the houses in Mohenjo-Daro were built to an identical rectangular plan, with fired brick walls and timber supports. Exterior windows and doors were rare, for reasons of security and for keeping the homes cool and free of dust. A single entrance door opened onto a side street. The houses were generally two-storied with separate rooms allocated to the family, guests, and servants. The inner courtyard was open to the sky; it was used for domestic tasks and for the children to play in. Wealthier houses had private wells, providing a constant supply of cool, fresh drinking water.

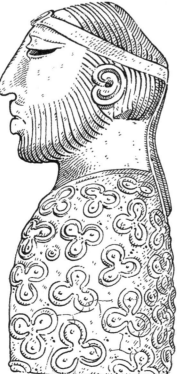

Male statues are rare in the Indus civilization, and the few specimens we possess represent men of importance rather than gods. This bust, carved in steatite, may be a king or a priest.

Many houses in Mohenjo-Daro had their own washrooms and lavatories. Fresh water was supplied to the houses through an arched brick tunnel (left). Once used, the water was carried to the main city drains through gutters at the foot of the house walls.

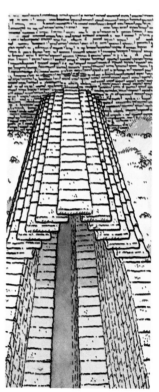

EARLY CHINA

In the fourth millennium B.C. the first agricultural communities were growing up in the lower basin of the Yellow River. From that point on, agriculture advanced steadily. The peasants took full advantage of the rich soil that was periodically covered with alluvial silt. They grew cereals (wheat and millet), and they also domesticated dogs, pigs, and later cattle and horses. They lived in villages of circular huts and made fine black and red pottery as well as stone and bone tools.

During the Bronze Age the first Chinese dynasty, the Shang dynasty, appeared. For five hundred years (between 1600 B.C. and 1100 B.C.), the Shang rulers, centered in the cities, established their dominion over the whole Yellow River valley. The king was surrounded by nobles who were in charge of warfare, politics, and religion. The cities they lived in were often very large, protected by enormous mud-brick walls. Only the nobility had the privilege of owning horses, chariots, and weapons. One of their duties was to protect the peasants who lived outside the walls. In return, the peasants provided the city dwellers with food, which led gradually to the development of an intensive farming system.

A great deal of emphasis was placed upon religious observances. No one built a house without consulting a priest or a geomancer for advice as to the most propitious site and position. Divination by fire was practiced by heating inscribed tortoise shells and the bones of sacrificial animals. The king used this method of guidance before making any important appointment, undertaking a military expedition, or setting out on a long journey. Ordinary citizens consulted oracles for all kinds of things—treating an illness, sowing the crops, and worshiping their ancestors. Unlike other people of antiquity, who used entrails for divination, the Chinese consulted only the bones of animals.

MASTERS OF BRONZE WORK

Bronze technology flowered during the Shang dynasty. Although the technology reached China after it reached the Near East, Chinese bronze casting rapidly reached an unparalleled state of artistry. The alloy used was 80–90 percent copper and 10–20 percent tin, with a minute amount of lead. Chinese smiths worked with nuggets rather than sheet metal. Among their finest pieces are a great variety of ritual vessels, each designed for a specific purpose. The vessels were given both geometric and animal decorations, as shown on this lid of a ritual vase of the thirteenth century B.C. (Guimet Museum, Paris)

The Shang emperor and his palace

The royal palace was the center of all activities in the Shang capital. The emperor, surrounded by noble advisors, governed his territory, led military expeditions, and made sacrifices to his ancestors and the great nature divinities—the gods of the sky, the earth, and the water. The Shang palace was 130 feet long and 40 feet wide; raised on a terrace of tamped earth, it dominated the whole city. It was not intended as a royal residence. With its four huge rooms leading to a series of corridors, and the four bronze ritual vases found there, it is more reminiscent of a temple where important ceremonies would take place.

The royal tomb of An-yang

The last eleven rulers of the Shang dynasty (there were thirty in all) lived at their capital of An-yang in Honan Province from the fourteenth to the ninth century B.C. Excavations of the city started in 1927, uncovering the remains of a 30-foot-thick wall, the foundations of rectangular buildings, and a great many tombs. In particular five graves containing chariots with their drivers and horses were found, along with some large tombs clearly intended for the emperors. One of the tombs contained not only the dead ruler's worldly goods (bronze bells, ritual vessels, pottery, and jade) but also horses, dogs, and most remarkably, a group of men whose beheaded bodies were carefully positioned around the royal coffin. They were very probably the emperor's companions and servants and the elite of his personal guard. They must have sacrificed themselves so that they could continue to serve their lord in the afterlife.

The first rulers of China

Several legends, included in the first Chinese historical documents, refer to the lives of the emperors who reigned in the predynastic period, in the third millennium B.C. They were all-powerful sovereigns, regarded as beneficent and civilizing influences on the country. FuHsi wrote the I Ching (The Book of Changes), Shen-Nung invented agriculture, and Huang Ti was the founder of medicine. However, archaeologists and historians have found no concrete proof that they ever existed, and they may have been mythical rather than historical characters.

THE WARRING STATES

According to the tradition laid down in the first Chinese historical records, the Shang dynasty disappeared in the eleventh century B.C., victim of ceaseless tribal wars and cities in rebellion. The Shangs were conquered by the Chous, a people from the Shansi mountains, famous for their brutality in warfare. The Chou dynasty founded two new capitals in the Wei Valley, Hao near Xian and Lo-yang in Hunan Province.

For a time the Chous upheld the ancient traditions of royalty they had inherited from the Shangs. At the top of the hierarchy was the emperor, the Son of Heaven, who held his power from the Lord on high; the emperor alone could carry out sacrifices in honor of the god. But in the eighth century B.C., some powerful cities, many a long distance from the capital, began to claim independence. Some of them, linked by family, business, or religious ties, grouped themselves together to form what amounted to principalities. In the seventh and sixth centuries B.C. their relationships maintained a peaceful balance in China. But as the years went by, they quarreled more and more often and the emperor lost his earlier powers of arbitration. The Chous themselves ended by being driven out of their western capital and received support only from the neighboring principalities. The Chous lost even this support in the fifth century B.C., and what was left of a centralized monarchy was broken up. It was the start of an era of ceaseless warfare known as the period of the Warring States.

During these civil wars the small cities of the central plain, which had inherited the oldest traditions, were absorbed by the powerful principalities that wished to extend their territory, increase their resources, and gain hegemony. There were six of these Warring States: Ch'in in the northwest; Hao, Han, and Wei in the middle Yellow River basin; the old, rich kingdom of the Ch'i, and, finally, Ch'u in the middle valley of the Yangtse. The fighting was ruthless. The soldiers of the most warlike kingdoms were only paid when they produced the heads of enemies. The civilian population was not spared, and when a town was successfully attacked, the whole population was killed, including women, old people, and children. Every now and then alliances would change, and the balance of power attained by the fighting was in a state of constant flux.

Enormous amounts of money were spent on equipping armies. Only the richest and best-organized states could afford to fight. The infantry, lancers, and traditional archers were joined by crossbowmen and horsemen, often equipped with war chariots. It was finally the cruelest but also the most energetic kingdom, the Ch'in, that conquered all its rivals. Its lord, Ch'in-Shih-huang, unified China in 221 B.C. and proclaimed himself First Great Emperor.

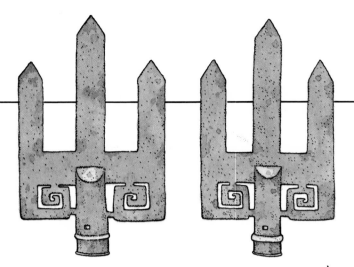

These great bronze symbols, 4 feet high, form the character shan, "mountain." They come from the tomb of Cuo, ruler of the small kingdom of Zhongshan, an ally of the Ch'i, destroyed by the Chous in 296 B.C. They were used to signal the august presence of the sovereign on the battlefield.

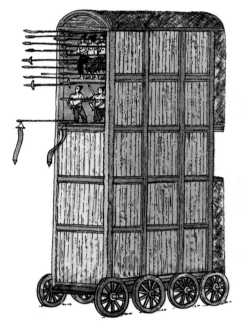

An assault tower owned by the Duke of Lu, from a Chinese engraving. The battles between the cities and the warfare between the Warring States were merciless. When the outcome was decided on the battlefield, towns would be besieged. As a rule, defeat meant the extermination of the entire population.

In the fourth century B.C. the crossbow made its first appearance. It had a bronze firing mechanism; when the trigger was pulled, the arrow was released with much more force than from a traditional bow.

Soldiers and their weaponry at the time of the Warring States. The weapons, made of bronze, were halberds, lances, daggers, and spears. Soldiers had helmets and shields for protection. Soldiers from wealthy states also had breastplates.

War chariots, drawn by one or two horses, were used for small skirmishes.

THE DAWN OF A GREAT EMPIRE

The Warring States period was not only a time of desperate fighting and bloodshed that tore China apart for two hundred and fifty years. It was also a time of great social change, which eventually led to the formation of a vast empire and a brilliant civilization.

Among the numerous technical innovations that stimulated a whole range of economic activities was ironworking. The Chinese were already skilled in metal working and were able to cast metal directly in molds, without having to go through the intermediate stage of forging. Agriculture was the first area to benefit; with iron implements the peasants could work the soil more deeply with less effort. They could also make lighter harnesses for their horses and thus get more work out of them.

Other agricultural improvements were the introduction of fertilizers, the draining of vast areas of marshland, and the irrigation of the fields by a canal system. So, despite the ongoing wars, more land was being cultivated.

Around the Yellow River a great deal of building went on; the work was placed under the authority of the kings of the states, which weakened the traditional power of the noble landowners. A series of reforms in the countryside allowed some of the peasants to own new land, and the old system of taxation imposed by the nobles was replaced by a direct payment to the kings of one tenth of the harvest. The kings, always anxious to add to the wealth of their states, put a tax on all agricultural produce and merchandise sold in the markets.

The great noble families were ruined, their lands taken over by the states. The nobles finally lost their political influence when civil servants were appointed to undertake the work of administration. The law laid the foundation for a new social order based on individual merit.

When the Ch'in kingdom emerged victorious, a centralized state came into being in which civil, military, and religious functions were kept clearly separate.

THE FIRST SCHOOLS OF PHILOSOPHY

Starting in the fifth century B.C., the political and social transformation of China was accompanied by new ways of thinking. The people who surrounded royalty at court included philosophers, who proposed governmental reforms and political principles. The first—and the most famous—was Confucius (551–479 B.C.). Having witnessed the decline of the nobility, he aimed to define the ideal of the "worthy man." Like his disciple Mencius later on, he insisted on the need for political action to be allied to morality. At the time of the Warring States, the most influential philosopher was Motzŭ (480–397

B.C.), who believed in universal love and pacifism. In the fourth and third centuries B.C., true political theorists, the Legalists, preached that the customs inherited from the past should be replaced by laws laid down by the state. Among them, Han Fei (280–233 B.C.) had a very important influence on the political development of China. Opposed to the Legalists were the Taoists, who preached individualism, detachment from materialism, and the poetry of the spirit. The most famous of them, Lao-Tzu, founded lasting religious and philosophical ideas.

A rich merchant carried in a chair

At the end of the Warring States period, merchants were becoming rich and influential citizens. They were happy to place their fortunes in the service of the state by investing in public building programs and financing the war effort. In return, they were given important posts. Some of the merchants became their rulers' most influential counselors; the Ch'in king who became the first emperor of a unified China appointed the rich merchant Lu Buwei as his prime minister.

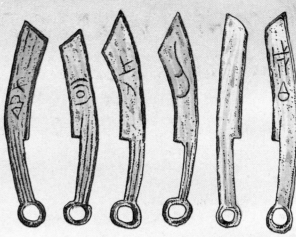

Money was used in China from the fifteenth century B.C. At that time, shells were used, pierced with holes so that they could be strung on a thread. In some regions this early form of money continued for 2,000 years. In the fifth century B.C. the first metal currency appeared in the form of iron blades or knives. In the Ch'in kingdom they were made by the state itself, but some of them bear the names of the town where they were issued, probably at the instigation of the merchants.

THE FIRST AMERICAN CITIES

The first inhabitants of America, who appeared some 60,000 years ago, had their origins in Asia. The flint spearpoints found almost everywhere in the northern part of the continent indicate that these people hunted big game like bisons and jaguars as well as smaller quarry like deer, hares, and birds. They also fished and gathered wild fruit.

Around 4000 B.C. the first plants were cultivated in Central America: first the squash, then beans and pimento, and finally—and most importantly—maize, a cereal obtained from a Mexican wild plant which was very gradually domesticated by the American Indians.

By about 3000 B.C. this form of agriculture was providing for people's daily food requirements, and several tribes were able to give up the nomadic life. The first settlements were built; communities were organized politically, economically, and socially. The regularity of the seasons allowed these early Americans to spend time on activities other than growing crops. Like the Asians and Egyptians of the same period, they improved their houses, clothes, and furniture and also invented pottery. Also like the Asians and Egyptians, the Americans very early on began to attach a greater importance to religion. Their priests tried to fathom the mysteries of plant life, invented myths about the creation of the world, and wove a series of rituals and sacrifices into daily life, aimed at creating close links between human beings and their natural environment.

Among the peoples who took part in this development, the Olmecs were in a central position. They were responsible for a remarkable culture that began to develop around 1500 B.C. Many features typical of the pre-Columbian civilizations made their first appearance with the Olmecs. Theirs was a large population that lived in settlements and had an intensive and flourishing agricultural economy based on maize. Unfortunately their houses were built with perishable materials and have all disappeared. They built ceremonial centers around large shrines, which contained pyramids and the famous "big heads" sculpted from huge single stones, as well as stelae and altars carved in relief and engraved with glyphs and even calendars.

At Tehnochtitlan, San Lorenzo, the foundations of more than two hundred houses have been found, which could have housed about one thousand people. But a very sizeable labor force must have been needed to build the great religious centers. The pyramid at La Venta required 200,000 tons of material. And the basalt blocks used by the sculptors weighed 10 to 30 tons each! How did the workers carry these blocks from the quarries in the volcanic region of Tuxtla, 75 miles away? There must have been an extremely powerful central authority capable of mobilizing thousands of people to take part—voluntarily or otherwise—in this great building program.

The Olmec culture died out around 500 B.C. for reasons unknown, marking the end of an important phase of American history.

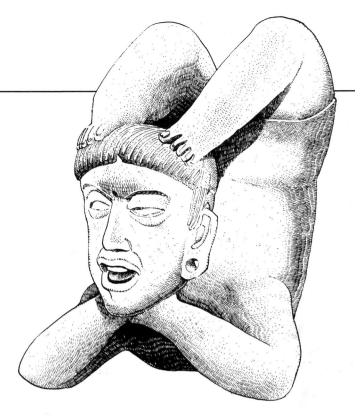

An Olmec statuette of an acrobat dating from the Pre-Classic or Middle periods (1200–700 B.C.).
Statuettes were usually female portraits; others represented shamans, jugglers, acrobats, and ballplayers.

One of the huge basalt heads found at the Olmec site of La Venta. It is 8 feet high and weighs 24 tons. It belongs to the Pre-Classic period (900 B.C.–600 B.C.) and is probably intended as an imaginary portrait of a powerful ancestor belonging to the Olmec elite.

The first Americans

According to current knowledge, based on geological stratigraphy and carbon 14 dating, humans may have appeared in North America 60,000 years ago. Although no one can be absolutely certain, most anthropologists agree that the first Americans were Asian in origin and would have crossed from one continent to the other by the narrow Bering Strait. All the indications are that at that time it would have been possible to make this crossing on foot over an isthmus in the seas of ice joining eastern Siberia to Alaska. America was then gradually populated from north to south. The oldest human settlements found to date are in Canada and California. Mexican sites date from about 25,000 years after that. South America, from the Andes to Argentina, was populated even later, some 13,000 years ago. From the great north to Tierra del Fuego, the migrations continued for six hundred generations. This slow expansion by small groups explains why there is such a variety of Amerindian cultures and languages. It is estimated that there were over two thousand languages on the American continent before the Europeans arrived.

Olmec sacrificial altar at La Venta. The crowned head seems to be emerging from the jaws of a stylized jaguar, an animal worshiped by the Olmecs. (Park-Museum de la Venta, Mexico.)

Olmec statuettes found in a tomb at La Venta.

THE ANDEAN CITY OF CHAVIN

The village of Chavin de Huantar is perched 10,500 feet up in the heart of the Andean cordillera in the north of Peru. The green slopes that lie at the foot of permanently snowcapped mountains witnessed the flowering of a major pre-Columbian culture. It lasted from the twelfth century B.C. until the fifth century B.C., when it came to a complete end. From Chavin it spread over a wide territory, from the highlands to the river valleys and the Pacific Coast. Chavin itself was a large religious center rather than a town. It never had more than a few hundred inhabitants, and the narrowness of the valley it lay in would have prevented it from expanding very much.

For nearly a thousand years, Chavin was a religious capital. Several times a year, ceremonies were held, made up of elaborate rituals and drawing crowds of believers from not only the nearby valleys but also even farther afield. Upon arrival the people gathered in the town center. Above them rose imposing buildings made of granite blocks, carefully cut and put together without mortar (like the Inca buildings that came later). Two temples dominated the scene—a stepped pyramid with a monumental door, and the temple of the Lanzon, a sacred shrine that contained a giant statue which was both feared and worshiped. The facades of the buildings were decorated with sculptures and relief carvings of the animals that played a role in their religious mythology—jaguars, serpents, and birds of prey like the eagle and condor. Inside was a complicated network of underground corridors and secret passages that could be used only by the priests.

It seems most likely that the pilgrims came to Chavin to consult the oracle in the temple of the Lanzon. The oracle was a terrifying statue, to which animals and, probably, human beings were sacrificed. It "spoke" to the crowd assembled on a platform outside the temple. An ingenious system was used to amplify the oracle's voice and make it sound terrifying. It echoed through the covered corridors, accompanied by all kinds of strange noises that came from underground canals fed by the nearby river. While all this was going on, the priests, whom the crowd had seen going into the temple, vanished into the secret passages and reappeared, as if by magic, at the top of the building.

The statue of the Lanzon, made in granite and placed in the heart of the temple, was nearly 16 feet high. It had a huge jaguar's head with menacing jaws. Above the idol was the sacrificial chamber. The blood of the victims dripped steadily through a drainage channel into the monster's mouth. The worshipers asked questions of the oracle that were in fact answered by the officiating priest, who lent his voice to the Lanzon and interpreted the results of the sacrifice.

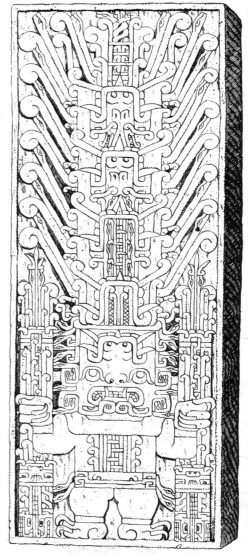

The "Raimondi stone," a stele found at Chavin in 1871 and examined by the famous Italian naturalist Raimondi.

It represents a divinity, with a mixture of human and mythical characteristics.

There are no texts to inform us about the religion practiced at Chavin, and no tomb has yet been discovered, so the meaning of the stone remains a mystery.

POTTERY

A typical example of pottery from the coastal region of the Chavin culture.

Starting in the eighth century B.C., the influence of Chavin extended far beyond its valley. Its beliefs and rites were adopted all over what is now Peru.

Chavin art was deeply religious, very often representing the culture's feline god in the form of a jaguar. Chavin pottery, sculpture, bone engraving, and goldwork herald the great artistic achievements of the Incas.

THE CITY THAT ROSE FROM THE SANDS

At the beginning of August 1933, near Abu-Kemal, a small Syrian town on the right bank of the Euphrates, some Bedouins were looking for large stones to place on a relative's tomb when they came upon a buried statue. They immediately notified the French authorities. (At the time between the two World Wars, Syria was under French administration.) An officer, Lieutenant Cabane, was sent to the site of the discovery, Tell Hariri (a tell is an ancient mound composed of the remains of successive settlements), to look at the damaged, headless statue. It represented a man with a naked torso, his hands folded on his chest, and it had a cuneiform inscription. After the statue had been dug up, Cabane had it sent to Abu-Kemal, together with a piece of terra-cotta tiling. He put a military guard around Tell Hariri to make sure that there would be no unauthorized digging and notified the archaeological authorities of the find. In Paris there was immediate interest. Since the statue could have been moved from elsewhere, its presence did not necessarily mean that Tell Hariri was the site of important remains. The piece of tile, however, was proof that a building had once stood there. Four months later, on December 10, 1933, André Parrot, an archaeologist, was sent to Tell Hariri by the Louvre Museum.

The steward and the miller

Parrot's first impression was one of disappointment, for the tell was not very large. It rose just a few feet above the sun-baked plain.

During the second excavation (1934–1935), André Parrot and his team began to explore the Palace of Zimri-Lim and came across the very fine statue of Ishtup-Ilum.

"At the foot of the tribune lay the statue of a governor (shakkanak) of Mari, Ishtup-Ilum by name, who was actually the builder of the temple of Dagan . . . Ishtup-Ilum, carved in basalt, a relatively hard stone, was delivered to us intact apart from a broken nose." (André Parrot, Mari capitale fabuleuse, Payot, 1974)

Nevertheless, a team set to work and carried out some careful initial excavations. Results were not long in coming. In January 1934 the team found three magnificent statues dedicated to the goddess Ishtar.

The first represented the steward Ebih-il, the second the miller Idi-Narum, and the third bore the inscription: "Lamgi-Mari, king of Mari."

The excavators all were convinced that under the small mound of Tell Hariri lay hidden Mari, the ancient city that had stood on the banks of the Euphrates.

Before the excavation, very little was known about Mari. From the little information that was available, it seemed that Mari had been the seat of a great dynasty. However, Mari was only mentioned briefly in a few inscriptions. These were more concerned with Mari's defeats than with its glory. It had been defeated by the troops of Kish and Lagash, occupied by Sargon of Akkad, and besieged and finally destroyed in 1760 B.C. by the armies of Hammurabi, king of Babylon. After this the archives said no more. Silence and the dust of centuries fell on

Rain and fire

During these fifty years of excavation, there have been quite a few adventures and incidents, some forming curious links between past and present. For example, on January 14, 1935, a violent storm hit the work area where the palace of Zimri-Lim was being dug up. When the storm was over, the team, worried about what a downpour of rain might do to the mud-brick walls, were astonished to find that all the water had run away through a drainage system beneath the palace, unseen but excellently designed. After 4,000 years the drainage channels functioned perfectly, just as in the days of Zimri-Lim!

Sometimes, too, archaeologists may benefit from what was once a disaster. When Mari was captured by Hammura-bi's troops in the second millennium B.C., the town and palace were ravaged by fire. This has turned out to be useful for archaeology, for the tablets in the archive rooms were baked and hardened in the heat, making them as durable as stone.

Mari; each year another layer of sand covered the remains of the ruined city.

At the beginning of the twentieth century, during a systematic exploration of Mesopotamia, archaeologists had certainly looked for some trace of Mari. Unfortunately they had ignored Tell Hariri, judging it to be too far from the Euphrates to be the location of the city.

Since 1934, when work first began on the site, twenty-four excavations have been carried out, interrupted by the Second World War and the 1956 crisis over the nationalization of the Suez Canal. The entire site has still not been explored, but the size of the discoveries and the amount of information they have yielded are unique in archaeological history the world over.

During the second half of this century the archaeologists have uncovered the great temple of Ishtar and the royal palace, with its 220 rooms, its courtyards, and its library containing twenty thousand tablets of archives. They have also found the ziggurat and numerous shrines, magnificent statues, mosaics, tombs, and the ramparts of the town.

When a site is opened up by archaeological excavations, the results are sometimes disastrous. Above, a courtyard of the Palace of Zimri-Lim in 1938; below, the same courtyard 35 years later, eaten away by erosion.

LIVING ARCHIVES

A culture based on writing was born at Sumer and within a few hundred years had spread throughout Mesopotamia. Other archaeological remains are silent witnesses of the past. By contrast, the thousands of tablets and inscriptions found at Mari, Ebla, Nineveh, Lagash, and Ugarit bring to life the actual voices of the people of those times.

The archives of these cities contain not only royal proclamations and great religious texts, but also a thousand and one details relating to everyday life. Ordinary citizens, as well as people of importance, inscribed (or got someone to inscribe) their acts and decisions and their joys and sorrows on clay tablets.

Translating and reading these archives takes one back 4,000 or 5,000 years in time, into the personal lives of the Mesopotamians.

Mesopotamian medicine

Extracts from the Treatise on Medical Diagnosis and Prognosis (eighteenth century B.C.)

A blow to the skull:
"If the person squints with both eyes, his skull has received a blow; and his reasoning powers are in the same condition as his skull."

An attack of fever:
"If, from the start, the sickness occurs in remittent crises, during which the patient presents alternate bouts of fever and then of shivering and sweating, after which he feels heat in all his limbs, and then finds himself taken with a strong fever, which next gives way to fresh shivering and sweating; this is an intermittent fever, due to a sunstroke—it will take him seven days to recover."

Epilepsy:
"If the person suddenly falls down while walking, keeping his eyes wide open, without bringing them back to their normal state, and if he is besides incapable of moving his arms and legs, this is the start of an epileptic fit."

Sicknesses inflicted by the gods:
"If the person is gripped by pains in the pelvic region, this has been inflicted by the god Shulak, because the person slept with his sister; he will drag on a little time and will then die." "If his temples are painful and his eyes veiled, it is because he cursed his own god or the god of his city." (Quoted by Jean Bottéro in *L'Histoire*, No. 74, pp. 21–23)

A remedy to apply in cases of "constriction of the lungs":
"Take . . . parts of a sheep's kidney, 0.5 ga of dates, 15 gin of turpentine, 15 gin of bay leaves, 13 gin of opopanax, 10 gin of galbanum resin, 7 gin of mustard, 2 gin of cantharidine. Pound these ingredients in a mortar with fat and dates. Turn the mixture onto a gazelle skin. Fold the skin. Apply it to the painful area and leave it for three days. During this time the patient shall drink sweetened beer. He shall take his food very hot and stay in a warm place. On the fourth day, remove the poultice." (Quoted by G. Roux, in *La Mésopotamie*, Ed. Seuil, p. 315)

Royal proclamations

Extracts from the Law Code of Hammurabi, King of Babylon (1760 B.C.)

On false witness:
"If a man in a lawsuit stands up to give evidence for the prosecution, and if he cannot justify his statements, if this case is a case of life [or death], this man may be condemned to death." (Hammurabi, 3)

On punishment:
"If a man has destroyed the eye of a free man, his eye shall be destroyed. If he has broken the limb of a free man, his limb shall be broken." (Hammurabi, 196–197)

On inheritance:
"If a man has given to his wife a present of a field, meadow, or house and has left her a tablet [a written document], after the death of her husband her children shall not contest anything; at her death the mother shall give it to the child that she prefers, but she shall not give it to a brother." (Hammurabi, 150)

A song of love

Extracts from the ritual Song of Love uttered by Kubatum, priestess of Uruk, during the new year ceremonies and addressed to her lover, King Shu-Sin (around 2030 B.C.):

Bridegroom, dear to my heart,
Goodly is your beauty, honeysweet,
Lion, dear to my heart,
Goodly is your beauty, honeysweet. . . .

Bridegroom, let me caress you,
My precious caress is more savory than honey,
In the bedchamber, honey filled,
Let us enjoy your goodly beauty,
Lion, let me caress you,
My precious caress is more savory than honey. . . .

You, because you love me,
Give me pray of your caresses,
My lord god, my lord protector,
My Shu-Sin who gladdens Enlil's heart,
Give me pray of your caresses.

— S. N. Kramer, *History Begins at Sumer*. (Philadelphia, Univ. of Pennsylvania Press, 1981).

Correspondence

Letter from Shibu to her husband Zimri-Lim, King of Mari (about 1780 B.C.):
"To my lord say this:
Thus [speaks] Shibu, thy servant. May my lord vanquish his enemies and then, safe and sound and joyful of heart, may my master return to Mari! And with this messenger a garment and a coat that I have made [myself], may my lord place [them] on his shoulder!"
(ARM, X, 17, *Correspondance féminine*, by G. Dossin)

When public building programs were started and towns founded, it was usual for royal proclamations to be inscribed on tablets or foundation stones. On one of these, Iahdun-Lim, king of Mari around 1900 B.C., declares: "[I], Iahdun-Lim, son of Iaggid-Lim, king of Mari, of Tuttul and the land of Hana, powerful king who controls the banks of the Euphrates. Dagan proclaimed my royalty. I built the wall of Mari and I dug its ditch. I built the wall of Terga and I dug its ditch. Moreover, in the burnt lands, in a place of thirst to which no king had given his name, where no king had built a town, I conceived a desire: there I built a town, I dug its ditch. Dur-Iahdun-Lim, I named it. Moreover, I opened a canal there which I named Ishim-Iahdun-Lim. I enlarged my land, I strengthened the foundations of Mari and of my land. Thus I made my name immortal. He who changes [the place of] my foundation inscription and puts [in its place] his own, that man, king or ishak [governor], may Anu and Enlil curse him with a terrible curse! May Shamash break his weapons and the weapons of his soldiers! May Ashnan and Shakkan bring famine to his land! The gate of his land, may it be seized by war! May conflict appear in his land! May his royalty be daily confronted by adversity his whole life long! May Anu and Enlil be evil demons for him for ever!"

The copper tablet opposite gives a similar account of the building of the capital of Sargon II of Assyria (721 B.C.–705 B.C.), together with curses on anyone who should destroy the works it commemorates. (Louvre Museum, Paris)

CHAMPOLLION AND THE HIEROGLYPHS

Although Greek was the language of the Macedonian dynasty founded by Ptolemy I in Egypt during the fourth century, a large majority of the Egyptian people kept their old language. Thus hieroglyphic writing continued to be used on temple walls and monuments. But demotic writing, although it lasted until at least the second century B.C., disappeared to be replaced by Coptic, a writing of the Egyptian language in a modified Greek alphabet that included some letters to represent sounds that Greek did not have.

Portrait by Léon Cogniet of Champollion in 1831. Only 41, he already had a lifetime's work behind him. (Louvre Museum, Paris)

Napoleon's scholars

On the banks of the Nile, the temples, obelisks, and colossal stone statues kept their mysterious inscriptions to themselves. For centuries no one thought of trying to read them. But then came the Renaissance, a time when people became interested in the languages and cultures of antiquity. A Jesuit scholar, Athanasius Kircher, was fascinated by hieroglyphs. In 1643 he realized that there was a link between Coptic and ancient Egyptian. Although his deduction was correct, the work on which it was based contained some wild inaccuracies. He made the mistake of attributing to hieroglyphs a symbolic value only, conveying ideas but not sounds.

His failure discouraged others from making similar attempts, especially since the few linguists at the time possessed only clumsy copies of the inscriptions on Egyptian monuments. More faithful copies were later brought back by scholars who accompanied Napoleon when he invaded Egypt in 1798–1799. They were collected and reproduced in 1809 in a series of volumes entitled *Description de l'Egypte*, making it possible to study them properly for the first time.

The most eventful discovery took place in 1799 at Rosetta, near Alexandria. During the digging of some earthworks, a French officer discovered a block of black basalt six feet high with three texts engraved on it. The first was in hieroglyphs, the second in demotic (ancient Egyptian cursive writing), and the third in Greek. When the Greek text was translated, it turned out to be a decree by Ptolemy V, the Macedonian king of Egypt who reigned between 210 B.C. and 180 B.C.

From 1802 onward several European scholars took on the task of deciphering the tripartite inscription. A Frenchman, de Sacy, and a Swede, Akerblad, worked on the demotic text, in which they were able to pick out the name of *Ptolemy*. In London an Englishman named Young studied the hieroglyphic text. He, too, identified Ptolemy's name, which was always enclosed in a cartouche (an oval frame), but he was unable to find any correspondence between the Egyptian signs and the Greek letters. At the same time, however, in Paris, Jean François Champollion was looking at a copy of the Rosetta stone . . .

The Rosetta stone
The famous black basalt stone was found at Rosetta in 1799 during Napoleon's expedition to Egypt. As a result, Champollion was able to decipher Egyptian hieroglyphs. (British Museum, London)

Champollion's death

On September 14, 1822, Champollion made a vital discovery. That day, he was sent some documents by a friend in Egypt, reproductions of the inscriptions on the temple of Abu Simbel. On one of them was a cartouche whose last three signs he knew well: an *m* and two *s*'s. Putting them together, Champollion saw that they resembled the Coptic word *mis*, "to give birth." With his remarkable knowledge of Coptic, he was able to deduce that the first sign, a drawing of the sun, could be read "Re" or "Ra." The result was *ra-mis-ss*, which was not only the name of one of the most famous pharaohs, Ramses, but could also be translated "Ra gave him birth"! Fired with enthusiasm, he ran to his brother's home, flung his notebook on the desk and cried: "I've got it!" But, overcome with exhaustion and emotion, he collapsed and remained in a deep coma for five days.

When he came to, he wrote a hasty letter to the French Academy outlining his theory and, to convince the skeptics, endorsed a complete translation of the Rosetta stone. He had ten more years to live, and he devoted them to a gigantic task of decipherment. He progressed with giant strides and in 1824 was able to start presenting a complete theory of the use of hieroglyphs. He established the fundamental distinction between phonetic characters conveying sounds, ideograms designating objects and ideas, and unsounded determinatives that conveyed grammatical instructions necessary to understand a sentence. In 1828–1829, Champollion fulfilled his dream of traveling throughout Egypt and verified all his claims on the spot, making a few corrections. He collected copies and transcriptions, which he included in two brilliant books, an Egyptian grammar and an Egyptian dictionary, published after his death on March 4, 1832. He was only forty-two when he died, but he had worn himself out with his life's work. Two months later, one of the two obelisks of Luxor arrived at the port of Toulon, a gift from Egypt to France. It was Champollion who had arranged for its transportation.

A fascination with the East

Champollion was born in 1790 at Figeac in southwestern France. From the age of fourteen he had a growing interest in Oriental languages. As a boarder at the Grenoble high school, he studied Greek and Latin and taught himself Hebrew, Arabic, and Coptic. At sixteen he entered the School of Oriental Languages in Paris, where he improved his knowledge of those languages and also mastered Syriac, Persian, Sanskrit, and Chinese. In 1810, already suspecting that hieroglyphs conveyed not only ideas but also sounds, Champollion began dedicating himself, body and soul, to the task of deciphering them. He was blessed with an exceptionally good memory and a powerful intuition, which were enhanced by his unusually methodic and disciplined intellectual approach.

After studying the Rosetta stone and other Egyptian documents, Champollion succeeded in picking out the name of queen Cleopatra (Cleopatra I; the famous Cleopatra, who was the last Macedonian ruler of Egypt, was Cleopatra VII) beside the word *Ptolemaios* (Ptolemy). The two names had several consonants and vowels in common—*p*, *t*, *l*, *a*, and *o*—which considerably added to his information. But he was convinced that the basis of the hieroglyphic alphabet thus obtained only applied to foreign proper names.

DECIPHERING INSCRIPTIONS

Hittite characters

In the twentieth century, deciphering an unknown language or script is still a hazardous undertaking. In spite of scientific progress and the now indispensable aid of computers, people who attempt the task have to go mainly by deduction, theory, and guesswork. They are like the wartime experts who decode secret messages sent by diplomats, officers, and spies. If they don't know the code, they have to discover what methods the writer used to conceal the original meaning. In this sense, decoding an ancient form of writing ought to be easier, since it was never intended to be impossible to read. But nearly 5,000 years of human history have so changed our ways of thinking, speaking, and writing that some of the techniques used in ancient times now seem impervious to modern logic and science.

Hittite hieroglyphs, carved in relief, formed beautiful decorations on the walls of palaces and temples. This superb stele decorates the entrance door of King Arara at Karkemish (on the Turko-Syrian border). Since Hittite writing was deciphered in 1939, we can read what it says: "Whatever the king who shall rule later over this town, if he plunders it by removing the stones or by removing the inscription . . . may the hounds of the god Nakarawa devour him!. . ."

Even so, there has been an enormous amount of progress due to the intuitive genius of people like Sir Henry Rawlinson who deciphered the British rock inscription of Darius I of Persia and Champollion!

These two pioneers, by deciphering the two great scripts of antiquity, Sumero-Akkadian cuneiform and Egyptian hieroglyphs, were able, among other things, to teach their successors a method of picking out individual linguistic characteristics that could be applied to unknown writing systems. This has helped several researchers who later managed to unlock the secrets of ancient scripts.

In 1930 the alphabet of Ugarit, in which a language near to Phoenician and Hebrew was written, was brilliantly deciphered by some French and German scholars. The writing of the Hittites, an Anatolian race who founded a large empire in the second millennium B.C., had for a long time resisted all efforts at decoding. The Hittites had learned cuneiform writing from the Babylonians and used it for their own archives. But the Hittites did not consider it appropriate for expressing their spoken language or for some of their ceremonial inscriptions. They were in frequent contact with the Egyptians, and from them they borrowed the idea of hieroglyphs but invented their own system. Their symbols represented parts of the human or animal body, plants, and geometric motifs, with two hundred signs in all, a quarter of which were phonetic. This double script disappeared in the seventh century B.C., when the last Syro-Hittite empire collapsed. It only reappeared in the nineteenth century, when several stelae were discovered in Anatolia and northern Syria. An Englishman, Sayce, was the first to study these strange signs, followed by Italian, American, Swiss, and Czech linguists. Their simultaneous and complementary efforts resulted in an acceptable translation in 1939. After the Second World War, the discovery of some bilingual inscriptions (Hittite and Phoenician) confirmed most of these interpretations; after that, it became relatively easy to read Hittite texts.

Glyphs and seals

The case of Cretan writing is more complex, for no fewer than four different systems appear in the few written records found on Crete! They have been classified into two main groups, hieroglyphic and linear, according to the appearance of the symbols. Each group is divided chronologically into two categories, A and B, A belonging to an older period than B does. Of the four scripts only the most recent, Linear B, has been deciphered. It was a laborious task, for almost all the inscriptions found relate to inventories and bookkeeping. Moreover, the system is very complicated, a mixture of a hundred or so ideograms with eighty-five syllabic symbols. An American woman, Alice Kober, found a pattern in it. But the actual decipherment was the work of two Britons, the architect Michael Ventris and the philologist John Chadwick. In 1953, aided by their expertise in ancient languages and a sound knowledge of mathematics, they managed to establish that the language written in Linear B was an archaic form of Greek spoken by the Mycenaeans who had occupied Crete.

Among the writings that still remain a mystery, the script of the Mayas presents enormous problems, for it does not seem to have been used for transmitting speech. The Mayan glyphs engraved on temple walls and stairways are twining figurative symbols which probably have a religious significance. Between the fifth and fifteenth centuries, the Mayans wrote numerous manuscripts; the manuscripts were, unfortunately, destroyed by the Spanish conquistadors, who regarded them as "words of the Devil." A unique survivor of this catastrophe is an astronomical calendar, which has given researchers an opportunity to study the mysterious symbols.

The ancient writing of the Indus Valley (2500 B.C.–1500 B.C.) is also a mystery. Written symbols appear on copper blades and chiefly on dozens of seals found at Harappa and Mohenjo-Daro and in Mesopotamia. The fact that there are at least three hundred symbols indicates that the writing was partly ideographic. Unfortunately, our total lack of knowledge of the Proto-Indian language, the small number of documents found, and the absence of a bilingual text prohibit, for the time being, any serious hope of deciphering this writing.

Etruscan script is another special case. The written letters were borrowed from the Greek alphabet and are easy to read. But the language itself is impossible to understand; Etruscan belongs to no known language group.

Tablet covered with Etruscan inscriptions (Villa Giulia Museum, Rome)

CHRONOLOGY

	Near East	Mesopotamia	Asia	America
−9000	Domestication of sheep.			
−8000	First wall of Jericho.			
−7000	Second wall of Jericho. First cultivation of cereals (barley, then wheat).			
−6000	Neolithic town of Çatal Hüyük in Anatolia. Start of weaving. Metalworking. Trade in obsidian. Domestication of cattle.	First agricultural colonies in Syria; village of Mureybet.		
−5000		First cities in the Tigris and Euphrates valleys: Hassuna, Samarra, Ubaid.	First agricultural communities on the banks of the Yellow River.	
−4000			Yang-shao culture in China.	Maize first cultivated in Meso-America.
−3500		First city-states: Eridu, Uruk, Lagash. Use of cylinder seals. Invention of the wheel and the potter's wheel. −3200: Birth of writing at Uruk.	Period of the legendary emperors of China. First cultivation of rice.	−3372: Start of the Mayan calendar.
−3000	Phoenician power in the Mediterranian.	First bronze tools. First dynasty of Ur. Gilgamesh, legendary king of Uruk. −2600: royal tombs of Ur.		
−2500			Long-shan culture in China.	Villages and towns in coastal Peru.
−2000		−2350: Reign of Sargon of Akkad. First written laws. −2100: Sumerian renaissance. Gudea, king of Lagash. Final decline of Sumer. −1860: Hammurabi, king of Babylon.	Birth of Indus civilization. −2100: Foundation of the semimythical Hsia dynasty in China. Decline of the Indus civilization. Foundation of Shang dynasty in China. First Chinese writing.	Valdivia culture in Ecuador.
−1500	Hittite empire in Anatolia. −1300: First alphabet at Ungarit.	Rise of Assyrian power.	Destruction of Mohenjo-Daro. An-yang, last Shang capital. −1100: Foundation of Chou dynasty in China.	−1200: Olmec culture in Meso-America.
−1000		Assyrian Empire	Decline of Chous in China.	Chavin culture in the Peruvian Andes.
−550			−551: Birth of Confucius. −453: Period of the Warring States. −221: Founding of first Chinese (Ch'in) empire	

Periods covered in this book

76

INDEX

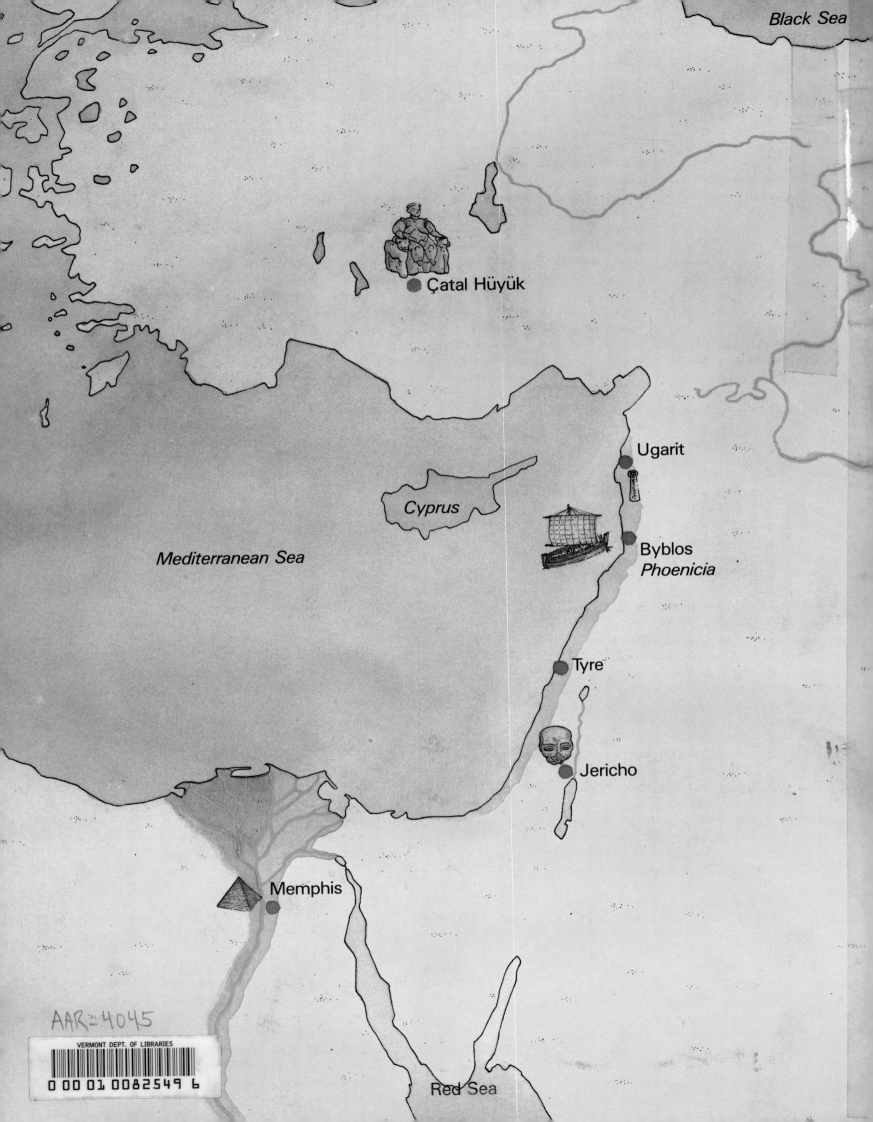

Black Sea

Çatal Hüyük

Mediterranean Sea

Cyprus

Ugarit

Byblos
Phoenicia

Tyre

Jericho

Memphis

Red Sea